WHAT OTHERS ARE SAYING

"Down to earth" and "grounded" are two of the most praiseworthy compliments one can receive. The outdoorsman way of life is alive and well in modern America, and most emphatically in the ranching lifestyle of the Great Republic of Texas. Kendal Hemphill deserves both of these compliments and verily reeks of this aboriginal down and dirty connection to the good mother earth. His writings exude the pure, organic reality of it all. Clearly allergic to all things politically correct, Kendal's humor, wit, and raw honesty provide a flow of refreshing reminders that the simple things in life are still the most important things, and that logic remains common and sensible. Take a breather and enjoy Kendal Hemphill.

—Ted Nugent

Even before I read Kendal Hemphill's book, I knew it would be full of it—"it" being Kendal's unique brand of wit and insight. I wouldn't take Kendal to the prom, but I would recommend reading him at every opportunity.

—Don Zaidle
Editor-in-Chief, Texas Fish & Game magazine

THE BUCK NEVER GOT HERE

THE BUCK NEVER GOT HERE

KENDAL HEMPHILL

Tate Publishing & *Enterprises*

The Buck Never Got Here
Copyright © 2010 by Kendal Hemphill. All rights reserved.

No part of this publication may be reproduced, stored in a retrieval system or transmitted in any way by any means, electronic, mechanical, photocopy, recording or otherwise without the prior permission of the author except as provided by USA copyright law.

The opinions expressed by the author are not necessarily those of Tate Publishing, LLC.

Published by Tate Publishing & Enterprises, LLC
127 E. Trade Center Terrace | Mustang, Oklahoma 73064 USA
1.888.361.9473 | www.tatepublishing.com

Tate Publishing is committed to excellence in the publishing industry. The company reflects the philosophy established by the founders, based on Psalm 68:11,
"The Lord gave the word and great was the company of those who published it."

Book design copyright © 2010 by Tate Publishing, LLC. All rights reserved.
Illustrations by Jim Swafford
Cover design by Kellie Southerland
Interior design by Jeff Fisher

Published in the United States of America

ISBN: 978-1-61663-123-9
1. Sports & Recreation, Outdoor Skills
2. Humor, General
10.03.23

DEDICATION

This book is dedicated to my wife, Jocelynn, who has borne my children, carried out my trash, cooked my meals, washed my clothes, ironed my shirts, cleaned my house, corrected my mistakes, screened my calls, folded my laundry, tolerated my friends, paddled my canoe, cut my hair, processed my dead game, patted my back, mopped up my spills, and put up with me in a million other ways during the twenty-four plus years we've been married. If she ever leaves me, I plan to go with her.

ACKNOWLEDGMENTS

There are a lot of people I'd like to thank for helping me produce this book. The following is a partial list, in no particular order:

Bill Clinton, Barbara Boxer, Ingrid Newkirk, Bobby Rush, Barack Obama, Rosie O'Donnell, Ted Kennedy, Dianne Feinstein, Robert Redford, Sheryl Crow, Ray Schoenke, Oprah Winfrey, Sarah Brady, Hillary Clinton, Nancy Pelosi, Alec Baldwin, George Soros, Bill Maher, Michael Moore, Barbara Streisand, Al Gore, John Kerry, Joe Biden, and Mike Farrell.

I would also like to thank whoever started the Greenpeace Movement, and the first vegetarian, and the guy who came up with the idea to use contraception as a way to control wildlife populations. I'd especially like to thank the fellow who first came up with the idea of duping the public with the threat of global warming.

If these space cadets had even the smallest, most tentative grasp on reality, my job would have been much harder. With their insane help, I've been able to point out the stupidity of gun control, animal rights, and the concept that using spray deodorant is going to destroy the planet.

To paraphrase Will Rogers, I don't make jokes, I just watch the people who 'care' and report the facts.

TABLE OF CONTENTS

Foreword 15

Introduction 17

Hunting 19

    Take A Shot At Muzzleloading 19

    Never Irritate A Mountain Man (Or Woman) . . . 22

    I Only Feel Sorry For The Doves 26

    Hunting Resolutions For The New Year 29

    The Fall Guy 33

Places 37

    Buddy, Can You Spare A Truck? 37

    Do you know the way to Monterrey? 41

    The dirty almost dozen: 46

    Forget Taco Bell–yo quiero Matacanes: . . . 50

    Anything Worth Doing,
          Is Worth Doing Tomorrow 54

    Pike's Peak The Beautiful 58

    Hicks From The Sticks 62

Animal Rights 67

    Animals Have Rights Too 67

    I Shot An Arrow Into The Courtroom 71

    Warning–Serious Column Ahead 75

Oil–A Slippery Issue 79

Wake Up And Smell The Decappuccino 83

Holidays 89

What Does Christmas Mean To You? 89

The Traditional Christmas Carcass 93

Nuts About The Indians 97

Intercepted Letter To Santa 101

Be Thankful You're Not A Turkey 105

The True Meaning Of Christmas 109

Kids 115

Vacationing In Colorado Is The Bearies 115

Boys And Bows–A Dangerous Combination . . 119

Kids–Our Hope For A Brighter Tomorrow 123

Boating 127

Tippycanoe And Nintendo Too 127

Bull Durham-Style Boat Building 131

Camping **137**

A River Runs Over It 137

George Washington Got Rained On Here 141

Fishing 147

Fly-Fishing—With A Cast Of Thousands 147

The Young Man And The Tank 151

Animals **155**

Never Let A Wild Animal
Back You Into A Corner 155

Living The Wild Life In The Suburbs 159

The Straight Poop On Bats 163

Guns 167

Gun Cleaning Made Difficult 167

Gun Cleaning Made Monotonous
  The Saga Continues 171

The Avalanche Has Started–
  It Is Too Late For The Pebbles To Vote 175

Bill Of Rights Or Bill Of Wrongs? 179

General 185

The Longest Distance Between Two Points . . 185

The Most Dumbest Invention Of All Time® . . 189

Breathing Oxygen Linked To Staying Alive . . . 192

A Plumb Good Idea 196

North America's Greatest Athletes 200

I Think I Could Be A Writer 203

Domestic Terrorists 207

A Convenient Lie 212

Author's favorites 215

Uncle Ray Wouldn't Have Wanted
  A Sad Tribute 215

Charly Mctee—The Voice Of Friendship 219

A Tale Of Two Flags 222

Dad 226

Just The Other Day 230

FOREWORD

Too many people in the world take things too seriously. They need to lighten up. And laugh. Life's rough, and if you can't find a little humor in it, you're doomed to a bitter existence, as are those around you.

My buddy Kendal Hemphill has been trying to do something about it most of his life. He's sort of a "Doctor Feel Good." He makes you laugh, even if it's at your own expense. Being around him is better for one's self-being than a subscription to *Psychology Today*. And it's cheaper. But not everyone reading his columns sees the humor in them. Some take Kendal–as they probably take life–a little too much at face value.

Jay Leno was not one of them when he read that Kendal had once written *"Breathing oxygen linked to staying alive."* Leno used that line one night on his show, giving Kendal credit.

A few might have thought Kendal was announcing his latest personal epiphany when he wrote the "oxygen" line. To those, he probably just gave that innocent, little boy look of his and went on his way, knowing you can't fool all of the people all the time.

Just some of 'em, some of the time.

—John Jefferson

INTRODUCTION

Outdoor writers fill a particular, narrow niche in journalism. Humor writers fill a different, but no less compartmentalized, spot. Outdoor humor writers don't really have a niche, as such. We're sort of like those guys that do the distance ski jump thing at the Olympics. There aren't many of us, and everybody else thinks we're nuts. But everybody also watches us, because they're secretly hoping to see the spectacular crash on the lower slope. Or something.

I didn't plan to be a writer; it just happened. It was sort of a fortunate accident, like when you're backing out of your driveway and run over the neighbor's cat, the one that always poops in your flowerbeds. It wasn't intentional, but you just can't help but smile at the result.

And then, since I fell into outdoor humor, it was like the neighbor was watching when you ran over the cat. Sure, you're happy the cat won't be spoiling your flowerbeds anymore, and I'm happy to have the chance to write, but you can bet someone is going to complain. Loudly.

But that's OK too. I figure if you're going through life without irritating people, you're just not trying hard enough. Some people need to be aggravated. Like people who allow their cat to ruin the neighbor's flowerbeds.

When I was in junior high, I had an English teacher who gave me an F on any paper in which I started a sentence with *and* or *but*. Now, every time I write a column, I start a sentence with *and* or *but*. And I get paid for it.

I also break plenty of other writing rules; not because I necessarily like to break rules, but because, like the guy who climbed the mountain, they're there. I end sentences with prepositions, I dangle participles, I use slang terms and double negatives. More writers should try it. It's fun.

And since facts are boring, I usually just make up my own. It saves a lot of research time, and gives me much more latitude. People usually don't know the difference anyway, because they don't care to do research any more than I do.

My main goal, though, is entertainment. I sincerely hope you're entertained by the columns in this book. And if you're not, I hope someone runs over your cat.

HUNTING

TAKE A SHOT AT MUZZLELOADING

If you're a little depressed about the end of hunting season, you may want to cheer yourself up by hunting during the special, antlerless-only muzzleloader season, which is available in many Texas counties January 9–17. Check your copy of the rulebook to see if your county offers this hunting opportunity, and if it doesn't, write your congressmen and senators immediately. Don't mention my name.

In case you're not familiar with muzzleloading-type weapons, they're kind of like guns, only different. As the name implies, a muzzleloader is loaded from the muzzle, or "powder horn" end, as opposed to a regular rifle, which is not. A regular rifle is loaded from the "breech," which is somewhere between the ends of the gun. Or else it is loaded from the bottom by means of a clip, which is punishable by a fifteen-yard penalty, or a magazine, such as the one you're holding.

Also, a regular rifle accepts a cartridge while a muzzleloader will always reject it, unless it happens to be a very attractive cartridge. The muzzleloader usually has to have the various components of a cartridge poured into it from the end. This is very dangerous, and must be done in a very careful and precise manner, in order to keep from blowing off a useful part of your anatomy, such as your noggin. "Never look into the end of your gun" was the number one mountain man rule of muzzleloader safety.

The components also have to be poured into the gun in a particular order. "Powder first, especially if there's Indians around" was another mountain man rule of muzzleloader safety. This is because if you decide, on a whim, to put your bullet in your gun first, there will be no powder behind it to shoot it out of the gun. The bullet has to be shot out of the gun because it is wedged very tightly in the barrel and has to be pushed in there with a gun stick, designed for that purpose, and known among muzzleloader enthusiasts as a "gun stick." Of course, your bullet may just roll freely down the barrel of your gun, in which case you have the wrong gun, or the wrong bullet, or both. This is because of calibers.

Calibers are numbers stamped onto the sides of all muzzleloaders. These numbers are very important because they designate the distance, in inches, that par-

THE BUCK NEVER GOT HERE

ticular gun will knock you backwards when you shoot it. In other words, if your muzzleloader has .45 stamped on it, when you shoot it, it will knock you backwards forty-five inches, or three feet, nine inches. If it says .50, then it will knock you back fifty inches, or four feet, two inches, etc. etc.

It's very important to match up the caliber number of your gun with the caliber number of your bullets. If they don't match, you will either get knocked back too far or not far enough. This is considered poor etiquette.

Anyway, if you poke your bullet down the barrel of your gun with your gun stick before you put your powder in, you won't be able to shoot it out, so you'll have to use one of the various methods available to remove it. All of these begin with being ridiculed by your peers for having forgotten the "powder first" rule.

After being ridiculed for a while, you'll have to attach a sort of screw onto the end of your gun stick, and then attempt to screw it into the bullet in your gun and pull it out. If this doesn't work, you can try another method to get the bullet out, but that method involves a part of the gun called a nipple, and I don't wish to discuss it in a family magazine.

I must mention the nipple anyway, however, since that's where you have to put the cap, in order to ignite the powder that you put in first. The nipple has a hole in the middle of it that leads from the outside of the gun to the inside, where the powder is. You have to put a cap, containing a small explosive charge, on the outside of the nipple, so when you pull the trigger and the hammer falls on the cap, the explosive charge will travel to the inside of the gun, ignite the powder, and blow the bullet out the front of the gun, which will, hopefully, be aimed at something besides your anatomy.

There's another type of muzzleloader called a flintlock, which doesn't use a cap, but a small pan full of powder next to your cheek. Shooting one of them is like trying to hold your gun steady while someone lights a blowtorch an inch from your eye.

Of course, we've only scratched the surface of muzzleloading in this column, and believe me, muzzleloading is glad. The point is that with proper instruction, you too can someday be an expert on muzzleloading, such as myself, and spend many happy hours being ridiculed by your peers...

NEVER IRRITATE A MOUNTAIN MAN (OR WOMAN)

In a recent column, I suggested taking advantage of the special muzzleloader season as a way to combat the post-hunting season blues. Due to the large number of favorable responses (one) that column generated, I decided to point out here that although the muzzleloader season only lasts a short time, the sport of shooting black powder can be enjoyed year round.

For instance, during the summer months, muzzleloader enthusiasts gather almost every weekend to engage in "shoots." Shoots are contests held at rifle ranges, wherein otherwise normal, sane people spend their leisure time causing permanent hearing loss to their friends.

Your first trip to a muzzleloader shoot will be quite an experience. These events are attended by some very colorful characters. You'll see people wearing fringed buckskin clothes, leather moccasins to their knees, and coonskin caps. Long hair and long bushy beards are common, with tobacco juice dripping down some of the beards. The men are even more colorful.

Besides wearing funny clothes, activities at muzzleloader shoots include leather tanning, knife and tomahawk throwing, flint knapping, spitting, scratching, building teepees, sitting around, building bows and arrows, and shooting black powder weapons.

Black powder people wear authentic, mountain man-type clothing and shoot authentic mountain man-type guns to recreate the atmosphere of the old-time mountain man jamborees held every spring during the early to middle 1800s, when mountain men came out of the mountains after trapping all winter. This was a time for celebration, and they mainly celebrated having managed to find their way out of the mountains, and getting through the winter without getting scalped by the Indians, who were largely anti-mountain man. In view of this fact, I've always wondered why teepees are erected at today's black powder shoots. It would seem that since Indians and mountain men were enemies, and Indians lived in teepees, mountain men would be opposed to having teepees at their gatherings. Of course, I've never asked about this, and if you know what's good for you, you won't either.

Actually, being able to find their way out of the mountains was no small feat for the original mountain men. The Boy Scouts of America organization had not been discovered yet, so there were no compasses. In order to figure out which way north was, the mountain men would make a small bowl out of birch bark, fill it with snow, and set it in the fire. When it started to boil, they would drop in a tuft of beaver hair and watch it swirl around in the water until it started to stink. Then they would gag, spit, and kick the bowl out of the fire. "We may be mountain men," they would say, "but we're not stupid enough to think you can make a compass out of a bowl of water." Then they would go back out of the mountains the same way they came in.

The yearly jamborees were an important part of being a mountain man, since the job held little opportunity for advancement. There was no "Head Mountain Man" title to acquire, so contests were held at the jamborees to see who was best at shooting, wrestling, spitting, whittling, hunkering, hawking, and killing Indians. These contests were eventually the downfall of the jamborees. Most of the mountain men quit coming when Jeremiah Johnson, played by Robert Redford, started winning all the contests every year. The other mountain men finally killed him and sold the movie rights to his story to MGM.

Being a mountain man was a difficult job, and the hardest part was probably loading those old muzzle-loaders. This was an extremely slow process, although with practice, many of the mountain men got so fast at it they could shoot four, five, sometimes even six shots a day with their rifles. The Indians they fought, however, primarily used the longbow, and they could shoot up to thirty arrows a minute. This may provide a clue to the fact that everyone who depended on the muzzleloader for protection is currently dead.

But being a mountain man had definite advantages, such as being your own boss. A mountain man could sleep 'til noon every day if he wanted, as long as an Indian didn't come along and scalp him while he slept. He also didn't have to worry about being hassled in airports by bald religious fanatics wearing sheets, or Amway distributors wearing suits.

The main plus to the mountain man lifestyle, though, was getting to spend a lot of time outdoors, which was fortunate, since mountain men were mostly trappers, and spent large sectors of their time with deceased animals. This, coupled with the fact that they hardly ever bathed, due to the freezing temperatures of most mountain streams, made them quite aromatic. This may explain why most of them were bachelors.

Though the mountain man disappeared a hundred years ago, due to corporate downsizing, his spirit lives on at muzzleloader shoots today. If you get the chance to attend one of these, it will be well worth your time. Just don't make fun of anyone's beard. Her husband may hear you ...

KENDAL HEMPHILL

I ONLY FEEL SORRY FOR THE DOVES

Mike Meitzel is your average, everyday overachiever. He's a freelance video producer from Vancouver, British Columbia, Canada. He's also an accomplished sailor who teaches celestial navigation, which is navigating by the stars, instead of using machines and satellites— almost a lost art these days. Mike spends his free time writing books about maritime history, and he has sailed all over the world. He and his wife home-schooled (boat-schooled?) their two kids a while back while they sailed the South Pacific for three years.

I met Mike a couple of years ago in Olney, Texas. He's a big, polar bear-looking guy (his hair is white) who smiles a lot and talks with a slight German accent. He's a hard fellow not to like. His list of "Been There, Done That's" would have made him impressive even without his friendly nature and quick wit. After sitting and talking with him a while, I completely forgot he was missing his right arm.

Mike was one of over two hundred amputees who were in Olney for the Twenty-Fifth Annual One-Arm Dove Hunt in 1996. The event is held the second weekend of September each year and draws eligible participants from all over the world.

It all started in 1972 with a couple of one-arm Jacks. Jack Bishop and Jack Northrup are a couple of guys who have, as they put it, "one good pair of arms between us." (One of them is missing his right arm, the other his left) They were sitting around at the coffee shop in Olney one day talking about dove hunting, and decided to hold a contest to see who could shoot the most doves. They got permission to hunt on a grain field near Olney and put the word out. Sixteen amputees showed up that first year, and the contest has grown by leaps, and of course bounds, ever since.

Scott Clark, who I met at college in Abilene, lived across the street from one of the Jacks and told me about the One-Arm Dove Hunt. Never having seen a one-armed dove, I decided to go to Olney and check out the event firsthand. I really don't know what I expected, but I remember thinking that, having both my arms, I might make some of the folks there feel self-conscious. I went determined to try not to embarrass anyone, especially myself. I needn't have worried. At the civic center, where most of the interaction took place, everyone went out of their way to make me and my family feel at home, especially the two one-arm Jacks.

The thing that impressed me most about the whole weekend was that while I met a lot of amputees, I didn't meet anyone who was handicapped, either physically or mentally, by their "after market alterations." I've never, before or since, heard so many jokes about missing limbs. And I heard them from people who were missing limbs.

Whenever someone made a speech, he would periodically ask for a round of applause. Those of us with both arms would clap, and everyone else would hold their hand out in front of them and wave it back and forth. The applause was generally pretty thin.

Once, while going through the buffet line during a meal, the guy in front of me was having trouble balancing his plate and tea glass with his one hand. Another guy walked up who was missing both hands, raised his leg up, and said, "Can I give you a foot with that?"

There was a large box on a table at the civic center that was marked "gloves." I asked about it and was told it was the glove swap box. Since gloves are sold in pairs, people with a right hand would bring their unneeded left gloves and drop them in the box, and then poke around in there a while. If they found a right-hand glove they could use, they took it. Left-handers would do the same.

Entertainment was provided by John Payne, the One-Arm Bandit and Company. John grew up on a ranch in Oklahoma and has been a cowboy and "Florida Cur Head Dog" breeder all his life, except for the one day when he tried to be an electrician. He got hold of 7,200 volts and held on to them for ten seconds. Besides some other damage, the jolt cost John his right hand. It also killed him, but CPR brought him back to life, and after recuperating, he went right back to being a cowboy.

John's show is an amazing display of horsemanship that would be impressive even if he had both hands. He's won the Professional Rodeo Cowboy Association Specialty Act of the Year Award five times. If you ever get a chance to see the One-Arm Bandit and Company, don't miss it.

The actual dove-hunting competition is divided into two categories: amputation above the elbow and below the elbow. In 1996, the winner of the above the elbow contest was Tim Wright of Georgetown, who limited out. The below the elbow winner was Craig Meier of Stephenville, who was one bird short of a limit. They both received brand-new Remington model 1100 shotguns. Craig gave his to his wife.

The first time I went dove hunting after that weekend in Olney, I tried doing it with one hand. It was, in technical terms, a lot of trouble. Now, whenever I start to feel sorry for myself, I remember that weekend, and I realize how easy I have things compared to some folks.

But I no longer feel sorry for amputees. They don't want my pity anyway and won't accept it if offered. Mike Meitzel summed it up for me when he said, "Losing a limb doesn't make people handicapped. They have to do that to themselves..."

HUNTING RESOLUTIONS FOR THE NEW YEAR

Did you ever wonder how the tradition of New Year's resolutions got started? Me neither. But since it's that time of year, I believe we, as outdoorspeople, should resolve to do something during the coming year to try to improve the image we have with the general public.

The reason I think we should try to improve our image is because, according to a recent survey I conducted among whoever I happened to run into recently, there's a widespread tendency among non-hunters to associate hunters with rednecks. This is, of course,

KENDAL HEMPHILL

about the dumbest correlation that can be made. Hunters are, in my humble opinion, the cream of society, while rednecks are marginally more socially acceptable than lawyers and congressmen.

I've studied this problem for quite a while (four minutes), and I've figured out why hunters are often grouped with rednecks. I've listed the main reasons here for your convenience.

1. Hunters and rednecks both drive pickups. Granted, most hunters' pickups are fairly nice and new, while rednecks' vehicles are generally old, beat up, and multi-colored, leaning heavily toward primer red and gray, and some are even multi-year-model. The differences are lost, however, on your average non-hunter. A pickup is a pickup, they believe, and all pickups look pretty much alike to them. They may even call pickups 'trucks.' This is another huge mistake, since a truck has eighteen wheels, and a pickup has four (six if it wants to show off).

2. Hunters and rednecks both spend a lot of time in the woods. Of course, hunters spend time in the woods because that's where the game is. They realize they have little chance of finding a trophy animal on a city street. Rednecks, on the other hand, spend time out of doors because of poor personal hygiene.

THE BUCK NEVER GOT HERE

3. Hunters and rednecks both wear silly clothes when they come to town. Hunters often wear camo to town, which is a mistake because of all the smells that can be absorbed into the material that make the hunter smell, to a deer, like a "sanitary" landfill. Rednecks wear their redneck clothes to town.

There are other things that may seem like similarities between hunters and rednecks, but these are the main ones. If you'd like a complete list, send me a self-addressed, stamped envelope and $500 cash, and I'll think one up for you.

But my point here is that as hunters, we most definitely do *not* want to be confused with rednecks. Being grouped with rednecks is a bad thing, because of the public image rednecks enjoy, and the fact that they enjoy their public image is an indication of their intelligence. Another indication is the fact that their two main spokespeople are (1) Bubba and (2) Jeff Foxworthy.

I've never personally met Bubba, and I don't care to. I have met a great many of his friends, and they're a strange bunch who do strange things, like ride mechanical bulls. This has always seemed to me to be one of the world's stupidest ways to waste a gob of time. The only thing stupider is riding a real bull, with a real temper and the added disadvantage of mobility, so that if you're still alive after he bucks you off, he can chase you down and gore you to death. Our society can disparage the ancient Romans for wanting to watch Christians get thrown into a ring with hungry lions, but an angry bull can be just as dangerous, and the Christians, at least, did not go into the ring willingly.

Aside from Bubba, Jeff Foxworthy is the most famous and revered redneck on the planet. I haven't been able to figure this out yet, because Jeff makes a lot of money making *fun* of rednecks. And they *love* him. They think he's the greatest thing since Bryl-Creme. They buy all his tapes, and most of them don't even have stereos.

I've never been able to understand this. Normally, when you make fun of a group of people, that group gets offended. If you make fun of Polish people, the Polish people get offended. If you make fun of Aggies, the Aggies get offended. If you make fun of lawyers, you get sued.

But Jeff makes fun of rednecks on national TV. He talks about how stupid they are, and how poor they are, and how badly they dress, and how many dogs they have, and they can't get enough. The only thing I can figure is that maybe the rednecks really *are* as dumb as Jeff says they are. Maybe they're too dumb to be offended when someone like Jeff makes fun of them. Or maybe they all think he's talking about all the *other* rednecks, but not them personally.

Anyway, for whatever reason, the rednecks all love Jeff, and he's getting rich off them, and they're not getting squat, except a bad reputation that they evidently want.

By now, you have forgotten my point, which is that we, as outdoorspersons, need to improve our image, so we will no longer be lumped in with the rednecks.

We can start by not wearing our camos to town. When you're hunting and you decide to go to town, take off your camos. This will take care of the silly clothes problem, but don't forget to put some other clothes on, especially if it's very cold.

Also, instead of pickups, we need to drive Suburbans, Blazers, Broncos, and Jeeps. This will set us apart from the 'rust and primer-' oriented rednecks. If you have a pickup, go out immediately and buy one of these other vehicles, and send me your old pickup. I'll dispose of it properly for you.

Lastly, to improve how people think of us, we need to work on our vocabulary. You can start by reading this column every week and using a dictionary to look up the words you don't know. And if I've used them incorrectly, please keep your criticisms to yourself...

THE FALL GUY

Bowhunting is one of the fastest growing sports in America today. It is also one of the most statistically dangerous hunting methods, coming in third behind (1) hunting Russian boar with a knife and (2) stalking mountain lion with a toothpick.

There are several reasons for this, first and foremost being the fact that a higher percentage of archers than rifle hunters climb trees. You may have heard the old saying that "what goes up must come down on a rock,

KENDAL HEMPHILL

or in a cactus patch." Bow hunters have been providing proof of this adage for years.

But falling out of a tree or elevated stand, while dangerous enough by itself, is even more dangerous when the faller has archery equipment in his possession. Landing on a quiver full of arrows can produce results far different from landing on a box of .30–06 shells. This is one of the main differences between hunting with a bow and hunting with a gun.

You should also never climb a tree carrying your bow and arrows, the way I do. Carry a small rope with you and tie one end of it to your equipment, and throw the other end over a limb of the tree you plan to hunt in. After you're in the tree, you can pull your bow up. Get down after your hunt the same way, only backwards. Duh.

Some of you, like me, ignore the danger and carry your bows while climbing. It's quicker and, as long as nothing bad happens, easier. It's also stupid. I can't follow you around in the woods and remind you that you shouldn't do this, so whenever you think about climbing with your bow, picture the old Carl Maulden commercials, where Carl puts on his frowny face and tells you not to leave home without your American Express card.

If you ever do find yourself falling with a bow in your hand, throw it. Bows are handy items, but they don't taste very good.

Another danger to consider when bow hunting is the fact that, on the front ends of all your arrows are small, double-edged knives. These knives are extremely

THE BUCK NEVER GOT HERE

sharp, or should be, anyway. If you decide to play Hiawatha and hunt with a back quiver, or any other type of quiver that holds arrows loosely, be careful where you step. Even a fall on the ground can pitch the arrows out of your quiver into the atmosphere, where your tender flesh is located.

I read about a hunter who tripped over a rock and fell forward, and an arrow from his back quiver fell in front of him and stuck in the dirt with the business end toward him, and ended up stuck through his calf. This can be painful at best, and fatal if the hunter is knocked unconscious in the fall and bleeds to death. Carl Maulden again.

Now for the helpful tips.

One thing you should remember while bowhunting is that you will need to be much closer to your game than when hunting with a rifle. Being close to your quarry will bring other factors into play, such as the fact that deer have much stronger senses than humans, and they can detect tiny movements, such as thinking. Don't think. Especially don't swat mosquitoes or gnats or flies. Be still. That's not easy when there are bugs chewing on your nose hairs, but it's necessary.

Deer can also hear much better than people. Consider the fact that you seldom hear does complain that their husbands never listen to them. Bucks listen to everything, including breathing, fidgeting, blinking, and stomach grumbling. Eat something before you go hunting so your stomach won't make any noise. Really.

It's also a good idea to blow your nose good before a hunt. Sneezing is not permitted, and it will not be tolerated by your prey. And if you've got tickly nose hairs, trim them. You never notice how often you scratch your nose until you can't.

Always carry a water bottle to your stand, since you'll need to be there for quite a while, at least an hour, before you expect deer to show up. An expensive canteen is not necessary and will probably leak anyway. I save twenty-ounce soft drink bottles, wash them out, and carry water in them. You can fill them to about 80 percent, freeze them, and have cold water most of the day, even when it's hot. For short trips, I keep some bottles about half full of ice and top them off with water just before I leave the house. Lean them a little in the freezer and the ice will freeze at an angle, and more of the water will contact more of the ice and get cold faster.

A half-full canteen sloshes and makes a lot of noise if you're trying to sneak up on game. You can avoid noise by squeezing a partly filled bottle until the water level reaches the top, and then put the lid on. You're going to throw it away after the hunt anyway.

Most canteens are fragile items, but there are exceptions. The Flex-i-Flask, from Temple Fork Outfitters in Dallas, is a limp canteen that can be put in the freezer without damage, and water can be boiled in it in a microwave oven. And it doesn't leak, which is rare for a canteen.

The handiest item to take bowhunting, as in any other pursuit, is common sense. Don't take stupid risks, and enjoy being outdoors. And above all, if you plan to fall out of a tree, don't forget your trampoline ...

PLACES

BUDDY, CAN YOU SPARE A TRUCK?

Last summer, my family and I went on a camping trip to the Frio River, below Garner State Park. We ended up spending two nights in a motel in Uvalde, when the Frio rose thirty feet in a few hours and stranded everyone in the area. It was quite an experience, and if any of you are planning to be involved in a flood, I highly recommend the Concan area. I've never been to a more impressive flood, or one that was more widely publicized or better attended.

One of the significant factors in our trip down there was that we didn't go in one of our own vehicles. Rule number one in flood attendance is never to take your own car. Many people who broke that rule ended up watching their automobiles floating away down the river. Being the paranoid fellow I am, I managed not to make the same mistake.

Toyota has a program, probably called the 'Driver's Side Windbag' program, that enables outdoor writers to borrow a Toyota for a camping or hunting trip, and all the writer has to do is mention Toyota in any story they get out of it. This is a very beneficial setup, at least for the writers, since most outdoors journalists are very poorly paid.

So when my wife and I decided to go to the Frio Flood, we called up the advertising agency of Hopkins & Associates, and arranged to borrow a nearly new, four-wheel-drive 4-Runner for the trip. (I should point out that, when we planned our trip, we didn't know it was going to flood, but I won't.)

The H&A people brought us the 4-Runner from Dallas and, a week later, came back and got it. The whole deal worked out so well I decided to call them up again the other day and see about getting a four-wheel-drive pickup for a trip I'm planning to go on in August. You'll be hearing about this trip again later, if I come back from it alive.

One reason I might not come back alive is that this little weekend getaway is being planned by my friend, Gordo. Another is our destination: Monterrey, Mexico.

Being a patriotic American and an ex-Marine, Gordo spends a good bit of his time running around in the woods, foregoing the pleasures of regular bathing and flush toilets, training as a National Guardsman. He spends one weekend a month and two weeks every summer preparing for the next war.

Being an out-of-shape American and a Lazy Person, I stay home and appreciate the fact that since Gordo is protecting the USA, I don't have to. I plan to spend the next war winning Pulitzer Prizes by reporting how it feels to be on the front lines, getting all my information from letters Gordo sends me.

Anyway, Gordo recently came home after spending his two weeks in the boonies at Fort Hood and told me we were going on an Adventure. I should have run the other way when he showed up wearing camouflage BDU's. Gordo's idea of an adventure is anything life threatening.

In the mountains near Monterrey is a river running through some pretty rough country, and some American INS Agents go there frequently to try to kill themselves. They've developed a sort of obstacle course involving mountain climbing, rappelling, caving, and floating down the river through caves and rapids and over waterfalls, with no boat. One of them, who happens to be in the National Guard, invited Gordo to come down and avail himself of the facilities, so to speak, and Gordo thoughtfully offered to take me with him. What are friends for?

The only problem with the whole deal, besides the coming back alive part, is that you have to have a four-wheel drive to get anywhere near the camping place. Neither Gordo nor I own a four-wheel drive at present, so I called up my old pals at H&A to see about getting a Toyota pickup for the trip. The lady I talked to was very helpful, and she was starting to fill out some sort of form for me when I mentioned Mexico.

Well. You'd have thought I'd told her I was planning to drive her pickup in a Demolition Derby the way she reacted. All I can say is the Toyota people don't seem to be trying very hard to promote international relations. They have some rule that you can't use one of their vehicles unless you promise to stay in the country with it. Which doesn't make a whole lot of sense to me, considering that most of the dadgum things are made overseas to begin with.

Anyway, this brings us back to the problem of coming up with a vehicle to go to Monterrey in. Gordo was counting pretty heavily on my being able to get a Toyota pickup, and now he's not too happy with me. And you don't want a big, bald-headed Marine upset with you, if you can help it.

So you readers are going to have to help me out. I figure somebody out there is bound to have a four-wheel-drive pickup, Blazer, or something they'll let us use for a weekend. It doesn't have to be especially new or fancy, and we don't care about a stereo or sunroof. For that matter, it doesn't have to have a roof at all, as long as it's four-wheel drive and will get us to Monterrey and back.

Now, I realize I'm asking a lot from you readers, but I promise to bring your truck back in the same condition it's in when we leave, provided the Mexican authorities have no objection. As compensation for the use of your vehicle, I'll write nice things about you in my column, and if that's not enough, I'll give you a check for, say, a million dollars. On Gordo's account.

So what do you say? Anyone out there willing to let your truck go on a genuine Mexican adventure? If so, let me know. And, if you don't mind, fill the truck up with gas before you bring it by. It's a long way to Monterrey...

DO YOU KNOW THE WAY TO MONTERREY?

*PART ONE OF THE MEXICAN
ADVENTURE SERIES*

BY SEÑOR KENDAL HEMPHILL

One of the main problems, as I see it, with having adventures in foreign countries is that you can't have them at home. But then, I guess if you could stay home and have adventures, they wouldn't be any fun. You could, however, at least speak the language.

Having decided to go to Mexico to see if we could run the Carrizo River and come back (especially come back) Gordo Gipson and I set out to try to get some other guys to join us. The only people crazy enough to go along were Gordo's brother, John, who lives in Dallas and therefore risks his life every day just driving to work, and Tommy Sullivan, who is a volunteer firefighter in Albany, Texas, and a lieutenant at the Abilene State Prison. Everyone else, when approached, backed away, eyeing us suspiciously.

We started off about ten o'clock on Friday morning, September 4, from Mason, and everything went quite well, I thought, until twenty minutes later when the transmission fell out from under Tommy's Explorer, which was expected to take us all the way to Monterrey and back. Clearly, this was going to be a long day.

We limped back into Mason in fourth gear, which still worked, and decided to take Gordo's Ford pickup and Mike Innis' Mitsubishi Montero, which Mike had, in a moment of weakness, offered to loan us for the trip if we needed it. We promised to bring it back in one piece, as long as the federales didn't have any objections.

We pulled up at the National Guard Armory in Laredo, Texas at about six that evening and met Paul Torres, who had caused all this trouble to begin with. He had invited Gordo to bring some guys and run the river, so everything bad that happened on the trip can legitimately be blamed on him. Paul told us to wait at the armory for Lonnie Colson, who would hold our hands and help us across the border into Mexico, in as much as he was a swell guy who had crossed the border many times. He was also the only other gringo on the trip.

Because of a mixup, Lonnie didn't get there until about eight thirty, and when we finally crossed Bridge One and met up with the rest of our group, it was after nine thirty Friday night. The others consisted of Paul's little brother, Adrian, a computer engineer from Nuevo

THE BUCK NEVER GOT HERE

Laredo named Ovidio Vazquez, Jorge something who smiled a lot, Juan something and his girlfriend, Veronica something, and Juan's father, who smiled all the time and was only catching a ride with us to the bus station in Monterrey. Ovidio, Jorge, Veronica, and Juan's father spoke very little English, which caused us to have to speak in capital letters with a Spanish accent when we addressed them, so they could understand us. In the parking lot outside Customs, I asked Juan's father, "El whereo is the el restroomo?" He smiled to show he understood and pointed to a middle-aged woman holding a goat.

Our real troubles began at the emigration area when we discovered we couldn't get a visa to go into Mexico with just a Texas driver's license, as some other form of identification was required to prove our u.s. citizenship. JC Penney underwear labels were not accepted. Luckily, Tommy had his voter registration card, but Gordo, John, and I had to come up with something to prove we were us.

Paul went with us back across the border into Laredo, afoot, to find a notary public, so we could get an affidavit of Texas citizenship based on our driver's license, which would prove to the emigration officials that we should be allowed into Mexico. I still haven't figured that one out.

We walked and waited and walked some more. Our search for a notary whose services were available after midnight on Friday, Labor Day Weekend took us over two hours. Finally, we located a cab driver named

Ruben Castillo, who was a notary, and he took us back to his office at the taxi service. He spent five minutes filling out four forms for us and charged us $25. We thought it was a real bargain and got a few of his business cards for future use.

When we got back to emigration, our affidavits of citizenship were accepted, but we were informed we would not be allowed to take Mike's Montero into Mexico, since we didn't have proof he had given us permission to drive it. Luckily we managed to get Gordo's pickup in, but it took another thirty minutes to talk them into that. While this was going on some people came by and asked us how to get visas without the proper papers. I gave them one of Señor Ruben's cards.

After spending about four hours doing what should have taken fifteen minutes, we went to Ovidio's house to leave the Montero, along with a lot of the gear we had planned on taking with us. Packed as light as we could manage, five of us got into Juan's Jeep Cherokee, three got into the front of Gordo's pickup, and four, including yours truly, piled in the back of the pickup on sleeping bags, making room for ourselves among the gear. We left Nuevo Laredo at two forty-five a.m., with almost five hours to go to our camping spot, where we had planned on spending the night.

Twenty-six kilometers south of Nuevo Laredo, as we neared the checkpoint where the Mexican customs officials usually catch the people smuggling guns and drugs, I asked Lonnie if I needed the papers I had been given at the border. He said I did, as the visa was my

THE BUCK NEVER GOT HERE

permission to be in Mexico at all, and without it I could be in real trouble. I had left my visa in the Montero, but luckily we weren't even stopped. I must admit, however, that the tension was very real for a few moments.

About twenty miles west of Monterrey, at a place everyone calls The Top, we left the blacktop and continued on a rough, narrow road full of tire-eating rocks. The road seemed, in places, to be in danger of coming unglued from the side of the mountain and falling a hundred feet or so into the tree-choked valley. I felt sure one of us would be bounced out of the pickup and fall, screaming, into the abyss. There was a sign nailed to a tree beside the road. I asked Adrian if it said to be careful or something, and he said, "No, it says not to wash your car in the river." He wasn't kidding.

As Saturday started to dawn, we watched the mountains appear, shrouded in mist, through breaks in the trees. About thirty minutes after we left the pavement, we arrived at our campsite at 'Ad Juntas' (the juncture), where the Rio Carrizo and the Rio Mauricio flow together. With three hours' sleep during the previous forty-eight, and half a roll of toilet paper, our real adventure was about to begin ...

THE DIRTY ALMOST DOZEN:

PART TWO OF THE MEXICAN ADVENTURE SERIES

BY SEÑOR KENDAL HEMPHILL

My friend, Ron Henry Strait, who writes outdoor stuff for the *San Antonio Express News,* is now on safari in Africa for a month. *The Express News,* for all I know, may even have paid his way and bought him new clothes and one of those neat jungle hats for the trip. I'll bet he even has a bunch of natives carrying his gear around the bush for him right now, and calling him "Bwana," and asking him if he needs more ice in his tea.

I, on the other hand, went to the mountains south of Monterrey, Mexico Labor Day weekend. I had to pay my own way, wear my own old clothes, and my own hat, and I had to carry my own gear. There wasn't much ice, but the people I was with did call me a lot of names, although 'Bwana" wasn't one of them.

Gordo and John Gipson, Tommy Sullivan and I were extremely impressed with the mountains, which are the tail end of the chain that includes the Rockies in Colorado; they just aren't quite as high. They do, however, contain the same picturesque, awe-inspiring beauty the Rockies are chock full of. If you drive carefully, you can get up to twenty oohs and aahs per mile.

Driving from our camping spot to the top of the mountain, Gordo seemed to be trying to break the

THE BUCK NEVER GOT HERE

land speed record for Number of Miles Driven without Touching the Ground. The road was about three feet wide and didn't go in a straight line for more than ten feet at a time. There was a nice, wide shoulder on each side of the road—unfortunately, they were vertical shoulders, one straight up and the other straight down. The road was full of the same tire-eating rocks all the roads in that area seem to be made of, and I got the impression the only thing holding it onto the side of the mountain was the bodies of previous travelers who had fallen out of their vehicles and gotten wedged between the trees below. Gordo compensated for his lack of vehicle control between periods of ground/tire contact by driving upwards of forty miles per hour. I've been assured that my most important bones can be reattached via major surgery.

We did finally get to the top of the mountain, where we found several log huts and barn-type structures, and some goat pens (although the goats ran loose along with the chickens and cows and dogs). A large family, including brothers, cousins, Grandpa, etc., lives in the houses, and makes their living by driving vehicles to the bottom of the road for idiots like us, at ten dollars per car. That and, of course, selling t-shirts for eighty pesos (eight bucks) each. There was only one design to choose from, but we all bought one because Lonnie Colson, our local guy from Laredo, said he'd been there twice before and hadn't gotten one. People snatch them up faster than Grandpa can haul them up the hill. They're status symbols.

The t-shirts say "Matacanes," which is the name of the route we took down the river. There's another route called "Hidrofobia," which contains a lot of technical rappels, and three people had been killed on that route the week before we got there, so we decided not to take it.

Matacanes (rhymes with "what the con is") means, literally, "Dog killer." The only thing I can figure is that it was named after the guy who supplies the meat to the café where we ate later.

We left our vehicles in the capable hands of the t-shirt salesman to be driven back down to Ad Juntas, hopefully not the quick way, and started up the trail to the beginning of Matacanes. The two-hour hike in the thin air was quite refreshing, and before long, I was so refreshed I could hardly breathe. When I asked how much further we had to go to get to the river, our leaders, Lonnie Colson and Paul Torres, must have thought I was upset that it was taking so long, so they started jogging. The hike turned out to be a little more taxing than my usual form of exercise, which is to get in a bathtubful of water and pull the plug and fight the current.

We finally reached the Carrizo at the top of an eighty-foot waterfall. After admiring the scenery for the requisite ten minutes, we hooked up our rope and rappelled down beside the waterfall, stopping on a ledge twenty-five feet above the water so we could jump to our deaths. We didn't actually die, but I could almost hear the water crunch on top when my feet hit it—it was so cold I forgot all about how hot I'd been while hiking up the trail.

THE BUCK NEVER GOT HERE

We all got down all right, so to compensate for this Ovidio Vazquez, a twenty-two-year-old computer engineer from Nuevo Laredo, promptly fell and cut a huge gash in his leg. We patched him up with a gauze pad and some tape, and he went the rest of the way down the river without complaint. About fourteen hours later, a doctor in the nearest town used several stitches to sew up the wound.

The actual trip down the river was a lot more fun than I expected, and I expected a lot. The course consisted mainly of huge rocks, sheer rock walls, overhanging vegetation, and freezing water. Matacanes is basically a ten-mile series of waterfalls on the Carrizo River, ranging in size from five to eighty feet, with rock walls and steep terrain hundreds of feet high lining the route. The method of travel we used was mostly to jump into the water at the waterfalls and swim across to the other side, and then get out and do it again. There was seldom any way to go around the river, as the terrain made this impossible.

The highest jump we made was about sixty feet, and it looked like a hundred from the top. The river is never wide, and we often had to be careful not to jump too far, lest we hit the rock wall on the other side. We didn't count, but I would estimate that we jumped into the water at least fifty-three thousand times that day.

The river also runs through two large caves on the route that could not have been avoided, even if we hadn't wanted to go through them. The first has to be rappelled into, as the water is too shallow to jump, though the rappel is only about forty feet. From there the cave gets dark, and the veterans made us leave our lights off and jump from the top of a twenty-foot waterfall in the dark. After that, there's a natural slide of about fifteen feet in the rock that dumps you back into the river, still in the cave.

The river finally leveled out at the bottom of a canyon, leaving us with a forty-five-minute hike over rough rocks to get back to Ad Juntas, where our eight-and-a-half hour ordeal came to an end. It rained on us for the last thirty minutes or so, and when we finally got back to camp, I could barely walk. I've never done anything more exhausting, or more fun. All eleven of us had made it down the river, but we still had a long way to go to get home ...

FORGET TACO BELL–YO QUIERO MATACANES:

PART THREE OF THE MEXICAN ADVENTURE SERIES

BY SEÑOR KENDAL HEMPHILL

When I tell people I went to the Sierra Madre Mountains south of Monterrey, Mexico on Labor Day weekend and rappelled, swam, and hiked down the Matacanes (dog killer) run on the Carrizo River, I get one of two reactions. One is, "Why?" and the other is, "Wow!"

Since I got back from Mexico, a lot of people in the first group have asked me why I would face death and

THE BUCK NEVER GOT HERE

dysentery, not to mention the very real risk of a lot of tax-deductible expenses, and go 250 miles south of the Rio Grande just to run a river. The only answer I can give is that no one who would ask that question would be able to understand the answer.

Actually, I wasn't sure what I was doing down there myself, by the time we had spent eight-and-a-half hours being cold, wet, and exhausted. I hadn't known it was possible to hurt so bad without dying. My body had grown several new muscles just so they could be sore. And to top it all off, it started raining half an hour before we got back to our campsite.

Luckily, the Adventure Club of North America had sent me three packets of a high-energy food-like substance called "Gu," and I had saved them for the trip to Mexico. They were each about twice as big as a trial-size tube of toothpaste, and the contents were about the consistency of toothpaste. I shared them with the rest of our group to get their reaction, and each of us squeezed a little out on a finger and ate it (the Gu, not the finger). The flavors were Vanilla Bean, Banana Split, and Chocolate Outrage, with the Vanilla Bean coming out as the overall favorite, although the Chocolate Outrage was at a distinct disadvantage, since I ate it all myself.

Anyway, after finally getting out of the river, we still had a few problems to work out. One fellow in our group, Ovidio Vazquez, had a four-inch gash in his leg that needed to be sewn up, and one of our vehicles had a flat tire and no spare, unless you count the small, tire-like device the car manufacturers are putting in cars these days in lieu of a real spare tire. So Paul Torres, Ovidio, and another guy named Jorge caught a ride, in the rain, in the back of a pickup for the hour-long trip to the nearest "town." They spent the night walking the streets, rolling the tire, looking for a doctor to tend to Ovidio's leg, and a service station that would fix the flat. They had managed to sleep for a good ten minutes by the time Gordo Gipson, Lonnie Colson, and Adrian Torres met them the next morning in Gordo's pickup to bring them back to camp.

While the rest of us had an easier time than the tire and leg crew, the night was no picnic for us either. Some of our group made their beds under a cabana by the river, which was a convenient spot for the mosquitoes to have supper. The building was about fifteen by twenty feet, and had a rough concrete floor and a metal roof, but no walls. We dubbed it the Hereford Hotel, since one of the free-ranging cows that dotted the area had wandered in and relieved herself in the middle of the floor. We wondered why no one had cleaned it up until we tried to find something to clean it up with. We ended up solving the problem the same way the previous occupants had—we put a table directly over it to keep from stepping in it.

It was about eleven o'clock that night by the time I got ready to change into some dry clothes, which I elected to do in the cabana, to keep from getting the tent wet and dirty. Everyone else had gone to bed, so I was the only one up when people arriving from

THE BUCK NEVER GOT HERE

upstream started coming to the cabana looking for Miguel, who had inconveniently gotten separated from his group on the river. Every time I started to take off my wet clothes, a new group would show up, most of them containing women, shining their lights around and calling for Miguel. None of them spoke any English, so I was forced to try to explain to them in Spanish that our cabana was not where the "patron" of the camping area was, and that my friends were trying to *sueño*. I did my best, but from the looks they gave me, I may have been telling them that I was the river's boss, and I had a live chicken in my shorts. By the time the third or fourth group had come by, John Gipson, from his sleeping bag, pointed out that I was making a lot of noise and suggested I walk down the river a ways and intercept the "Miguel seekers" before they got to the cabana so he could get some sleep. They finally gave up on Miguel, and I went to bed.

The next morning, Tommy Sullivan went looking for a *banyo* (restroom) and found an outhouse near the cabana. It consisted of three, very porous, see-through tin walls and a door opening (with no door) facing the river. He declined.

The tire and leg crew finally got back about noon, and we packed up and started home. Riding in the back of Gordo's pickup on the way back, Lonnie, Tommy, and I figured out a way to make history. Since Matacanes means "dog killer," we decided the next time we run the river, we'll take a Chihuahua with us. If he makes it through, we'll dress him up in a little life jacket and shorts and put a headlamp on his head and take his picture. We'll have a bunch of t-shirts made up with his picture on them with a caption that says "Forget Taco Bell, Yo Quiero Matacanes," and sell them at the river. That is, unless Taco Bell comes up with a large cash contribution toward our next trip to Monterrey...

ANYTHING WORTH DOING IS WORTH DOING TOMORROW

Probably the most important and most overlooked aspect to consider when planning a physically taxing outdoor activity is the physical condition of your very own physical body. Too many otherwise pleasant outings have been cut short, and almost ruined, when one or more of the participants have died from overexertion. To keep this from happening to you, you should make it a point to get yourself in shape before going outdoors and killing yourself.

Several years ago, I heard about a couple of friends from Texas, Sam and George, who had always wanted to play golf at the Augusta National Golf Course. They finally got the chance to go, and the evening of their first day there, Sam called his wife.

She asked him if he was having fun, and he assured her the trip was a dream come true. He told her about their hotel, and the beautiful golf course, and the friendly people. She asked how he had played, and he told her he'd done fairly well, scoring in the high eighties. She asked what George had shot, and Sam said, "Well, George didn't actually finish the round."

Sam's wife pressed him for details, and he finally told her that George had had a heart attack and died on the seventh green. She was aghast and expressed grief for George. She also offered sympathy to Sam for having to go through such an awful experience. "You must be drained," she said.

Sam answered, "I'll say. For the last eleven holes it was hit and drag George, hit and drag George ..."

This tragedy could have easily been avoided, and we can all learn a lesson from it, namely—never play golf with someone who has a bad heart without first renting one of those electric carts.

I've been thinking a lot lately about how out of shape I am, since Gordo and I are about to go on another trip into the Sierra Madre Mountains near Monterrey, Mexico, and traverse the Carrizo River again. Our first encounter with the Matacanes (dog killer) run down this river, last Labor Day weekend, was one of the most enjoyable experiences of my life, and I think it would have been even more fun if I had not been breathing so hard the whole time that I couldn't straighten up. Some of our fellow adventurers told me the scenery was magnificent, and I'm sure it was. I wanted to look at it myself, and I would have if I hadn't been so busy leaning over with my hands on my knees, wheezing, staring at the patch of scenic Mexican dirt between my blistered feet.

I hope to have an easier time on our next trip (which is set for Memorial Day weekend) and maybe walk upright at least part of the time, so I decided recently that the time had come to buckle down and force myself to actually start a rigorous program of thinking about getting into shape. I put it off as long as I could, as I agree totally with the attitude of the famous person (I forget who it was) who said she wasn't very interested in working out, and that her attitude was "No pain, no pain."

For the last ten or fifteen years, I've tried to keep my body's caloric ignition to a minimum because of my strongly held opinion that if I were just going to burn the calories up anyway, there was no point in going to all the trouble of ingesting them in the first place. The most vigorous exercises I participate in on any kind of a regular basis are scratching, belching, and yawning. If I want a really tough workout, I'll sneeze two or three times in a row, or try to scratch the spot between my shoulder blades that's so hard to reach, without rubbing my back on a doorframe.

This regimen has suited me fairly well, since it has the advantages of being easy to maintain while not being very difficult to maintain. The only problem with it I can see is that it hasn't perceptibly done me any good. Although this is a shortcoming I am completely comfortable with in an exercise program, I finally decided that if I planned to spend eight and a half hours hiking, climbing, rappelling, and swimming in an atmosphere almost devoid of oxygen, I would have to adopt a more strenuous approach.

So I finally took the bull by the horns, struck while the iron was hot, made hay while the sun shone, put

THE BUCK NEVER GOT HERE

my nose to the grindstone, threw the baby out with the bath water, brought home the bacon, and allowed my mouth to start writing checks my body couldn't cash. That's right, I actually got busy. I sat right down with a pencil and a piece of paper and worked out a new exercise program for myself.

My new routine included some very radical maneuvers, such as sit-ups, push-ups, chin-ups, running up and down stairs, breathing hard, and falling facedown on the ground. Once I figured out exactly what exercises I planned to do, and how long I had for my new workout schedule to get me into shape, I was very proud of myself. I also figured that if I stuck to it even after the trip and didn't wimp out, I would end up looking like Arnold Schwarzenegger in only about two hundred and fourteen years, give or take a decade. I was all ready to get started making myself miserable.

Then, as luck would have it, I had a stroke of luck. I was channel surfing on the television one evening and came across a program about visualization. I learned that, contrary to the natural laws of nature, a person can actually make himself taller just by closing his eyes and *imagining* he is taller. I had never heard of such a thing, and I was very impressed.

So then I thought, "Well now, if I can make myself taller through visualization, how come I can't get myself into better shape the same way? Huh?"

So that's my new plan. Every evening I sit for fifteen minutes and imagine I am virtually indistinguishable from Jean Claude van Damme, except for being more literate. I think it's going pretty well, although I hardly ever smile anymore, and I look half-asleep all the time, and people are always coming around wanting me to fight. Barring any unforeseen problems, I hope to go on TV in a month or two and tell everyone about my new, pain-free workout. I should make a fortune, provided people can still understand what I'm saying ...

PIKE'S PEAK THE BEAUTIFUL

When Katherine Lee Bates gazed out at the view from Pike's Peak in 1893, she was inspired to write the poem "America the Beautiful," later put to music and now known, for some reason, as the song, "America the Beautiful."

When I gazed out at the view from Pike's Peak in 1999, I was also inspired to write "America the Beautiful." Unfortunately, I was 106 years too late. I didn't have time to worry about it, though, because I was too busy yelling at my three boys to stay away from the edge. Colorado is an ideal vacation destination for young boys, who derive some sort of sadistic pleasure from teetering on the edge of one abyss or another while their parents yell at them to back up. The optimist may look at Colorado and see mountains; the parent looks at the state and sees abysses.

Pike's Peak was named for the man who discovered it in 1806, Lieutenant Zebulon Pike's Peak. Zebulon had come to Colorado under orders from the U.S. Army, not only to spend some of your great-great-great-great-grandparents' tax dollars, but also to explore the area and see if there were any decent ski resorts around. He located Vail and Aspen, but he neglected to mention either of them in his official report, due to his disgust in finding them inhabited mainly by snobby, blond, preppy college students with names like Biff and Buffy.

Zeb and a small party of men tried to climb the mountain that November, but only got about ten thousand feet high, due to the fact that the road was under construction at the time. He predicted that no one would ever climb to the top, and that Katherine Lee Bates would write "America the Beautiful."

My family and I decided to climb Pike's Peak by way of the Cog Railway, since the only other option, except for walking up, was to drive up the road, which is still under construction. Our decision was also influenced by the fact that we were driving a Jayco motor home, and had become so attached to it that we didn't want to drive it over the edge of an abyss. Further, we knew we would have to return the motor home at some point, and we didn't want to have to pay for it, especially if it was at the bottom of an abyss.

The Manitou and Pike's Peak Cog Railway is the highest of the fifty-five rack railways in the world, and has the greatest elevation gain—7,500 feet. The idea to build a railroad up the mountain was inspired by the poem "America the Beautiful."

Just kidding. Actually, the railroad was inspired by a mule ride up the mountain in 1889. Zalmon Simmons, who owned a mattress company in Wisconsin, had ridden a mule to the top of Pike's Peak and was sitting in a hot tub when he decided to write "America the Beautiful." He also decided he wanted to go back up the mountain, but he never wanted to ride a mule again. So he financed the Manitou and Pike's Peak Railway Company, and hired a bunch of unskilled laborers at twenty-four cents an hour. Several of them were killed in blasting accidents, which inspired Katherine Lee Bates to ... right. Anyway, the railroad was finished on October 22, 1890.

The ride up in the train, for the most part, involves a lot of swallowing and yawning to clear your ears, and looking out the window at trees, which appear to be leaning at a forty-five-degree angle. Luckily, we sat near a nice family from Holland, consisting of Henny, Marianne, and ten-year-old Arjen van Os. My Dutch is a little rusty, but Henny knows enough English to get along, and we had a lot of fun trying to talk to them. Arjen spent most of the ride teaching our boys how to say some Dutch words, and since coming home, we've corresponded with them via email and learned that, after seeing the view from Pike's Peak, Marianne was inspired to write a poem entitled "America the Not Too Shabby."

What surprised me most about Pike's Peak was not that automobile and motorcycle races are conducted on the road to the top of the mountain, or that people actually *pay* to be allowed to ride a bicycle *down* this road. There are plenty of idiots in the world, and many of them can be found fooling around near large abysses, trying not to fall in. What surprised me most was that every August, a marathon is held on Pike's Peak road.

THE BUCK NEVER GOT HERE

People who I'll describe as "not nuclear physicists" race up and back down the road, a distance of twenty-six miles. And the record time for this race is three hours and twenty-four minutes, which inspired the winning marathoner to fall face down on "America the Beautiful."

While I'm not a marathoner, I like a challenge now and then, so when I got home from Colorado, I pointed out to my friend, Gordo, that if a string bean in a pair of nylon shorts could run up Pike's Peak and back in three and a half hours, a couple of fine specimens like ourselves should be able to do it in two days. So that's what we plan to do, in the spring of 2000, provided Colorado is still there after the great Y2K disaster. And in order to make things interesting, I decided to invite my favorite humorist, Dave Barry, to come with us. Dave, while he pretends to be a wimp, actually has participated in some pretty strenuous activities, including rappelling, snorkeling, laser tag, parenting, and driving in Miami.

Then Gordo, who often bites off more than I can chew, decided we should challenge Dave to get a team together and race us up the mountain. I thought that sounded like a really stupid idea, but I agreed due to the fact that if we fall behind, Gordo will have to carry me.

So what do you say, Dave? Interested in a little contest here? Or are you chicken? Remember, an opportunity like this comes along once in a lifetime. If you're lucky...

HICKS FROM THE STICKS

People often call me up and say, "Kendal, you being such a smart person and all, can you tell me where I should take the family for vacation this year? Well?"

When this happens, I usually tell folks the place to go for the ultimate family trip is Sioux Falls, South Dakota. Not only does Sioux Falls have one of the largest populations of black flies in the u.s., but it also boasts the added attraction of the only sewage lifter in the country named after Dave Barry. No kidding.

So, while a bunch of dweebs spent their vacations in the Midwest, my family and I went to Washington D.C. When I figure out who got the better end of the deal, I'll let you know.

We decided to go to D.C. because (a) we wanted our children to get an idea of how our government works, (b) most of the really neat stuff to do in D.C. is free, and (c) we have friends living in the area, so we didn't have to rent a hotel room.

Our friends, Joel and Julia Gonzales, live in McLean, Virginia, just across the Potomac River from D.C. Julia is a Lieutenant Colonel in the u.s. Army, and works at the Pentagon, which is where all the important military decisions are made, such as what color the carpet should be in the office of the Commanding General at Fort Bliss, in El Paso.

During the two days we spent being tourists at our nation's capital, Julia's mother, Peggy, played tour guide for us. We rode the subway into D.C. both days, partly

THE BUCK NEVER GOT HERE

because hardly anyone ever gets killed on a subway anymore, and partly because our nation's capital was not built to accommodate the turning radius of a Chevrolet Suburban. We never did find a parking space big enough, and we never saw another Suburban, or even a pickup, in D.C.

The first place we went was the Smithsonian National Museum of Natural History. As we walked up to the door, we discovered that my eleven-year-old son, Courtland, was carrying a fairly large lock-blade knife. We decided not to take it away from him, assuming a boy would get into less trouble than an adult if caught with a knife. Besides, we have two other sons.

Luckily, the knife was not discovered, and we were able to go inside. The Museum of Natural History is very impressive and contains lots of attractions, such as the Hope Diamond. Personally, I was not all that impressed with the Hope Diamond. I thought it would be bigger. At about forty-five and a half carats, I suppose you could use it to knock someone out, but you'd have to swing it pretty hard.

In the same room with the Hope Diamond is a Mason County blue topaz, which was donated by someone named Chamberlain. As I was standing there looking at it, a fellow walked up beside me, so I told him I was from Mason County. He looked sort of confused and hurried away. City folks can be a little rude sometimes.

At noon, we decided to eat at the Atrium Café, which is in the basement between the Museum of Natural History and the Museum of American History. The food was not bad, but I think the Atrium Café is attempting to pay off the National Debt with its proceeds, judging by the prices.

We spent the afternoon in the Museum of American History, where we saw lots of neat old stuff, such as the Fort McHenry flag that inspired Francis Scott Key to write the 'Star Spangled Banner,' thus damaging the vocal chords of millions of American school children for generations to come.

At another building, we saw the "Ground Zero Flag," the one the firefighters raised over the rubble of the World Trade Center on 11 September 2001.

We spent the entire next day at the Smithsonian Air & Space Museum, where most of the nation's used air and space is kept. Hanging in the lobby is the Wright Flyer, the Wright Brothers' plane which made the first heavier-than-air flight. Not a model. The real plane. Also hanging in the lobby is the Spirit of St. Louis, in which Charles Lindberg made the first solo flight across the Atlantic Ocean, and the Bell X-1, "Glamorous Glennis," in which Chuck Yeager broke the sound barrier. Not models. The real planes.

The lobby of the Air & Space Museum also contains the pod in which John Glen became the first American in space, the pod from which Ed White made the first American space walk, and the pod from which Neil Armstrong became the first man to set foot on the moon. And that's just the lobby.

THE BUCK NEVER GOT HERE

We also got to see the Lincoln Memorial, the Vietnam Memorial, the Korean War Memorial, and the Memorial Memorial.

The highlight of our trip to D.C. was the Tuesday evening ceremony at the Iwo Jima Memorial. The Norwegian King's Guard, including his band, performed for us. The Norwegians have a silent drill team, and they aren't too shabby.

Then the U.S. Marine Band came out, followed by the U.S. Marine Silent Drill Team. For years I've wanted to watch the Silent Drill Team. It was better than I expected.

The whole Marine Guard, probably 100 of them, marched around impressively for a while, and then a group of about thirty came out front and center. They all twirled their fourteen-pound Garand rifles around like batons, and then stopped and stood still like a line of statues.

The CO, with no rifle, marched down the line and stopped in front of a marine who had taken the bayonet off his rifle. The marine then went through a routine of fancy twirling, ending up flipping the rifle from behind his back to the CO. The CO caught it, inspected it, twirled it around a while, and then flipped it back and marched on down the line.

It looked like the show was over, but as the CO was marching down the line, another marine flipped his rifle to him. He caught it in mid-stride and stopped in front of a third marine. The CO again went through his inspection and twirling, and then went through the twirling and flipping routine with both marines number two and number three at once.

The whole performance was doubtless the most impressive thing I've ever seen. There were probably several thousand people watching, and no one made a whisper through the whole show. If every American got a chance to see it, there would probably be a lot fewer flag burnings.

I had planned to straighten out the budget deficit problem while I was in our nation's capital, but unfortunately ran out of time. I would highly recommend a vacation in Washington D.C., but you really need more than two days, so you can work in a trip to the Kendal Hemphill Memorial Sewage Lifter in Arlington, Virginia...

ANIMAL RIGHTS

ANIMALS HAVE RIGHTS TOO

A friend recently alerted me to an article that said the average cost of saving a seal after the Exxon Valdez oil spill in Alaska was $80,000. Two of the most expensively rehabilitated seals were released back into the wild at a special ceremony, and as they swam away, they were loudly cheered and applauded by the onlookers present. Before they got out of sight, however, they were eaten by a large killer whale.

Those of you who are, at this moment, saying, "Awwwww, how saaaad," would do well to skip the rest of this column and go play with your poodle. This article is for the rest of you, who are laughing so hard you are leaning over drooling on your leather shoes.

I usually try to avoid writing columns that contain a lot of facts and information, especially if any research is involved, since research is boring. But lately I've been learning quite a bit about animal rights groups without even trying, and I feel obligated to pass some of this information along to you, not out of any sense of moral duty, but out of my deep-seated need to come up with a column containing about a thousand words.

My education about the bunny huggers started when I was poking around on the internet and found a website that contained an animal rights section. Now, I should stress right here that I am a strong advocate of animal rights. I believe they have the right to be fattened up good and eaten. They have the right to remain silent. They do not have the right to an attorney, although quite a few have been appointed for them, especially by a group called the Animal Legal Defense Fund.

Anyway, I had always known there were animal rights activists out there but, since I've lived all my life among normal humans, who raise cattle for food, hunt deer, etc., I had never really thought much about them. They were just sort of out there, somewhere, like people who buy the polyester pants you sometimes see in stores. They didn't bother me, and I didn't bother them. Finding a listing of animal rights groups on the internet, however, was an enlightening experience. Although I'd rather have stayed in the dark, I found that there are a lot more of these people than I thought, and they're out to get me.

For instance, there is a group called the Hunter Saboteurs Association, which distributes information about how best to go out and find people who are hunting and fishing (legally) and scare off the fish or game so it won't be killed. They try to teach their converts how to do this unobtrusively, since they know it's illegal, but they also inform their members on how to act if caught and arrested, so they have a better chance of avoiding prosecution.

Another group calls itself Defenders of Wildlife and claims to pay ranchers at full market value for any loss attributed to predators. I doubt it will do you any good, but some of you ranchers might want to file claims with this group the next time you lose livestock to coyotes. Their website address is: www.defenders.org.

The World Society for the Protection of Animals spent a tubful of money a while back sending some of their people to Honduras after the recent flooding down there, but not to help the homeless, starving people. No, they went there to aid the animals victimized by the disaster, setting up shelters and food banks for displaced pets and other animals. I guess their motto could be "Save the cats, let the people starve."

The website for peta (people for the ethical treatment of animals) has a Question of the Week section, and one of the questions I read there was, "If everyone in the world quit eating meat, would there be enough plants to feed everyone?" peta's answer was that we feed animals "80 percent of the corn we grow and more than 95 percent of the oats," to fatten them up for consumption. So if we stopped eating animals, everything would be hunky-dory.

I sent peta an email and asked them, basically, if the animals that are alive now already eat most of the grain we grow, and we quit eating animals so there are soon a lot more of them running around fruiting all over the plains, eating more of our grain, how did they figure there would be plenty of plants for us humans to eat? Huh?

They wrote me back and said that I shouldn't worry, that they had studied the situation and figured it would work itself out, since people who raised animals for food would raise fewer animals. Somehow I doubt their accuracy, but I let that one go.

I also sent an email to the Defenders of Wildlife, who have worked real hard to save American wolves from being wiped out by you rich, greedy ranchers just because they eat your livestock. I told them I was all for saving the wolves, but I was worried about all the little bunnies and rats and such the wolves eat. I got a message back that said I should talk to peta about it.

The Hunter Saboteurs Assoc. has not responded to my query about the two occasions in the Bible when Jesus fed fish to crowds of people.

Two people, however, have exchanged messages with me about a claim made on peta's site that Jesus was a vegetarian. One of them, who I believe is a peta employee, has respectfully and intelligently tried to straighten me out, although all his arguments are wrong. When I pointed out Genesis 9:1–7, he claimed the Bible has been translated incorrectly. I figure Bill Clinton feels the same way, and thinks the seventh commandment should read, "Thou shalt commit adultery."

The other person started out kind of friendly and said that everyone knows Jesus was a vegetarian. When I, politely and respectfully, pointed out proof that this wasn't true and urged her to look things up for herself, she accused me of provoking her and trying to push my opinion on others.

I don't think I was able to change anyone's mind, but I haven't given up entirely. Somewhere in the world, there must be an animal rights activist with some common sense, and I'd love to sit down and discuss the issues with him or her ... over a big, juicy deer steak ...

I SHOT AN ARROW INTO THE COURTROOM

One of the main problems I have as an outdoor humor columnist is writing something interesting without irritating anyone. I sometimes have a hard time seeing the other person's point of view, since I'm always right. Ha, ha! Just kidding! Actually, everyone thinks they're right, and I'm no exception.

This being the case, I'm always surprised when someone disagrees with me. I guess I shouldn't be, since it happens so often, but obviously not everyone can be as smart as me.

For instance, the editor of *Texas Wildlife* magazine recently received a letter from a Dr. Thomas G. Murnane, Interim Executive Director of the Humane Society of North Texas in Fort Worth. Dr. Murnane took umbrage at a suggestion I made in a recent magazine column concerning sharpening one's bowhunting skills. To be specific, I said that people who live in cities could use stray cats and dogs for archery practice.

Dr. Murnane wrote:

> "The article is intended to be humorous. However, the author's reference to practicing on stray dogs and cats is repulsive and insulting to your readers whose mentality and sensitivities I trust are above those of the author and editor who permitted this passage in your magazine."

Well. You'd have thought I'd poked fun at Elvis. I guess I could have just assumed Dr. Murnane was one of those humorously challenged people who can't take a joke, but since he pointed out that he knew the column was supposed to be funny, I prefer to believe he's a featherhead. No offense, Dr. Murnane. By the way, why are you so stingy with your commas?

Anyway, after studying the situation for a while, I've decided to try to point out a few things about my columns that may not be quite as obvious as I thought they were.

1. The views and opinions put forth in this column are not necessarily those of the owners or editors of whatever publication this column appears in.

THE BUCK NEVER GOT HERE

2. The views and opinions put forth in this column are not necessarily those of the author of this column. I make these stories up, without regard to truth or accuracy, and my research usually consists of cleaning my fingernails and drinking a glass of tea.

3. Nothing in any of my humor columns can be taken even remotely seriously. For instance, if I were to write a column explaining the best way to field dress a deer, I might say the first step is to run him through the washer on spin cycle with an old pair of boxer shorts. This is, of course, ridiculous. Everyone knows briefs work much better.

4. I never use stray cats or dogs for target practice. I did shoot a chicken once, but I had the express written permission of the owner, and the chicken was taken in fair chase, more than fifty feet from the henhouse.

Having said all that, I hereby make formal apology to Dr. Murnane, the Humane Society of North Texas, and stray dogs and cats everywhere, from the bottom of my heart, liver, kidneys, and of course, spleen. I should not have suggested shooting at strays, and I will henceforth be more careful what I write.

The Humane Society is an honorable organization and should be lauded for the tremendous efforts it makes. I'm not real clear on what those efforts are, but I am quite sure that efforts are made, and good ones too. Of course, the argument could be put forth, if someone felt like arguing, that the tremendous efforts of the Humane Society could be redirected to better use in the area of, say, curing world hunger, under the pretense that people are more important than animals. Actually, hungry people in some parts of the world, Asia for example, might be happy to have the thousands of strays the Humane Society "puts to sleep" every year since cats and dogs are, to those folks, food. (You might say they like to "wok" the dog.)

Now, I'm not suggesting we send strays out of town to become entrees, no sir. I think putting them to sleep is the best way to go, and I don't think we should stop with strays either. I think we should go ahead and gas dogs that bark all night at nothing, cats that poop in my children's sandbox, and any dog that jumps up on people with muddy paws. If we're going to treat these animals with the respect they obviously deserve, I think we should demand the same respect from them. And while we're at it, let's go ahead and whack those little poodles that look like sculpted shrubs. They'd probably call Dr. Kevorkian themselves, if they had opposable thumbs.

Actually, I've always been very benevolent toward strays, and even adopted a stray dog and cat while I was in college, even though pets were specifically proscribed in my dorm. My cruel, heartless resident assistant managed to get rid of the dog, but the cat just kept coming back, even when the RA repeatedly threw it out the third-floor window.

Many of you reading this column are probably hunters; others of you are landowners who earn part of your living by leasing your land to hunters. The end result of a successful hunt often involves killing an animal. But there is a whole lot of difference between killing a deer or turkey and killing a wild dog or cat. I don't personally know what that difference is, but if you're vague in that area, you should check with Dr. Murnane. I'm sure he could clear the question up for you in a jiffy.

Not, again, that I advocate the senseless killing of strays. The Humane Society sensefully puts them to sleep, so there probably aren't a lot of them in your area anyway.

The problem remains, then, of what to use for target practice. My new and improved suggestion: lawyers. There are more of them than there are strays, they're bigger and easier to hit, and they're easy to find; all you have to do is follow the sound of the sirens.

Now if we can just find a country where the people use lawyers for food ...

WARNING–SERIOUS COLUMN AHEAD

In a recent column, I suggested using stray cats and dogs for archery practice. In the same article, I pointed out that nothing in any of my columns should be taken seriously, but evidently, a great many people did just that. I've been getting a lot of feedback from that column, mostly from people who enjoyed it. A few people have even invited me to engage in archery practice in their neighborhoods. But, in fairness to my detractors, I must point out that not everyone loves me unconditionally.

One woman came into my office and berated me personally. She went on at length about how wrong it was to kill any animal, and how she was a vegetarian, etc. She was wearing a very nice leather jacket at the time. She also admitted eating eggs, which is, in effect, killing chickens.

Deer hunting, she said, was reprehensible. I pointed out that our ancestors who came to America before HEB was invented killed deer to eat. She allowed that was true, but that they didn't enjoy it. Obviously, she is also clairvoyant. Retroactively.

This woman represents a small percentage of the population of Texas, but they happen to be a pretty loud bunch. I suppose they ignore the fact that, even though hunters harvest a lot of deer every year, a good many still die of starvation during the winter-because the food supply is inadequate to support even their decimated numbers. I haven't interviewed any deer, but if you gave me a choice between being shot and starving to death, I don't think I'd need a lot of time to think it over.

Which brings up another problem with anti-hunters—when a deer habitat is taken over by humans, greater numbers of deer are crowded into smaller spaces. I agree this is true, but I have a solution. Humans who are worried about this to the point that they want to do something about it should move to Pluto, which

THE BUCK NEVER GOT HERE

is appropriate since it is named after a dog. This will accomplish two goals. It will slow the encroachment of humans into animal habitat and keep the rest of us from having to listen to them bellyache about something that's not a problem.

The reason this is not a problem is that there are thirty-six times as many white-tailed deer in the United States now as there were in 1937. Thirty-six times. There are also forty-five times as many wild turkeys, nineteen times as many rocky mountain elk, and eighty-three times as many pronghorn antelope now as there were in 1937. I didn't make these figures up. I got them from the news branch of the Texas Parks & Wildlife Department.

Franklin Delano Roosevelt signed the Federal Aid in Wildlife Restoration Act on September 2, 1937, to fund wildlife management and research programs, hunter education programs, habitat acquisition, and wildlife management area and shooting range development. These projects are managed by state wildlife agencies, and they're funded by (anti-hunters are asked to please sit down now) an 11 percent excise tax on firearms, ammunition and archery equipment, a 10 percent excise tax on handguns, and hunting license proceeds. Since inception, $3 billion have been raised from these taxes, and $1 billion from hunting license sales. Which means hunters are responsible for the vast increase in the numbers of wild animals roaming the purple mountains majesty and fruiting on the plains of America.

Of course, anti-hunters have probably done a lot for wildlife too. Off the top of my head, I can't think of a thing, but if you give me a few decades, I'll work on it. In the meantime, I believe antis should be allowed to park in handicapped parking spaces.

I guess it's hard for some people to understand how we can love and respect an animal and hunt it at the same time. That's difficult to explain, but my friend, Bob Warren, of San Antonio, has written a book that I believe illustrates the feelings hunters have better than any other book I've read.

The title is *How Could You, Danny?* and it's about a girl from the city who goes to visit her cousin in a rural area, and is appalled to learn that he hunts. During her visit, she comes to understand that her uncle, a veterinarian, and his family have a deep respect for animals and don't compromise that respect by hunting. The book is written on about a fifth-grade level and teaches ethics and moral values concerning hunting as a sport. I recommend it highly for anyone interested in hunting, on either side of the issue.

Ethics and morals, I believe, are a serious problem in our country today. A person who robs an egg from the nest of bald eagle faces a $5,000 fine, and while I think that is appropriate, it is ludicrous in view of the fact that a doctor can legally open up a human baby's head while it is being born and vacuum its brain out to kill it. This is called "partial-birth abortion." Twice, the house and senate have passed a bill to ban partial-birth abortion, and twice President Clinton has vetoed the legislation.

This type of thing demonstrates that we, as a nation, value animal life above human life. Folks, that's wrong. I don't believe any more than anyone else that animal abuse is acceptable, but it's not a drop in the bucket compared to child abuse. If we don't learn now to value our children, we have no future as a nation.

As difficult as it may be to believe, I never purposely try to offend anyone. My columns are normally meant only to amuse. To some, my sense of humor may seem inappropriate. For that, I apologize. However, I will never apologize for hunting and playing my small part in a program that has so greatly increased the numbers of game animals in America. Before you come and shake your finger at me, get the facts. No one does more for animals than hunters.

Yes, our wildlife is important, nay, vital, to our country. But without hunters, our wildlife is doomed. And without our children, we are doomed …

OIL–A SLIPPERY ISSUE

Unless you live on the planet Goober, you've smelled the big stink over oil and gas exploration in ANWR, the Arctic National Wildlife Refuge. The tree- and bunny-huggers have their synthetic socks in a wad because George W. and company want to open part of the area to drilling. The earth-first genre are claiming the oil companies will irreparably damage the tundra, kill the fish, force the caribou to quit migrating to their traditional calving ground, emotionally disturb the polar bears, and no telling what else.

The question of development versus environmentalism has always been interesting to me. It's obvious there has to be a balance between intelligently making use of our natural resources and preserving those same resources for the future. Everyone knows that if you eat the goose, you don't get any more golden eggs.

Now, I like goose as much as the next guy, but I have to admit there is a limit. Responsible stewardship dictates that we follow game laws, respect private property rights, and use some common sense. The trouble is that common sense is so uncommon these days.

In order to make a sensible decision on an issue such as drilling in the ANWR, it is necessary to get the facts. I am normally opposed to facts, on the grounds that they are often boring and difficult to acquire, but since this is a special case, I decided to put myself out. I was not much surprised by what I learned.

The state of Alaska contains 365 million acres, populated by about 640,000 people, which translates to almost a square mile per person. This is a difficult amount of area for most folks to wrap their minds around, especially those living in an apartment in Washington, D.C.

The ANWR is a 19.8 million acre chunk of northeastern Alaska that is mostly a flat, treeless bog. The temperature often drops to forty degrees below zero during the winter. Average summer temp is a balmy forty above, warm enough for abundant mosquito production. For some odd reason, there is not a long line

THE BUCK NEVER GOT HERE

at the travel bureau full of folks wanting to visit the ANWR. Go figure.

GW wants to allow oil type exploration in a 1.5 million-acre chunk of the ANWR, which is about 8 percent of the entire ANWR range, and less than 0.5 percent of the total area of Alaska. For perspective, consider that Alaska is over four times the size of Texas. And there are a lot more oil wells in Texas than in Alaska.

But when we get right down to the nitty gritty, it really doesn't matter much what you and I think about oil exploration in the ANWR. The people who should be allowed to decide are those who will be most affected, the people who live there.

Yes, people live there. There is one town in the ANWR, Kaktovik, perched precariously on the edge of the Arctic Ocean, on a stretch of beach about as far north as it is possible to go and still be in the United States. Population: 293, not counting sled dogs. Over 80 percent of Kaktovik's residents are Inupiat Eskimos, hardy people who live pretty much off the land and sea.

The city of Kaktovik conducted a survey to determine what the locals thought about oil and gas exploration in their backyard. Sixty-eight people were consulted, a huge percentage of the population, as surveys go.

Over 90 percent of Kaktovikians participate in hunting and fishing, including the harvest of whales. A whopping 16 percent live entirely on harvested game, and another 58 percent say more than half their food supply comes from the land and sea. So it would be reasonable to assume that preservation of the area's natural resources, particularly the wildlife, is very important to these folks.

The loudest battle cry of the environmentalists against drilling in the ANWR is their complaint that the 175,000 caribou living in the area will be run off from their traditional calving grounds, and will therefore no longer bear young. When asked about this possibility, 41 percent of the locals said the caribou would not be affected at all. Only 18 percent said the caribou would leave the area, and none thought it would harm the animals.

Almost three quarters of Kaktovikians said the quality of their lives will be diminished if oil development is stopped, and that they are satisfied with the environmental practices of the oil industry on the North Slope. They named improvement of schools, health care, job opportunities, and recreational activities as advantages afforded them by the oil industry.

Only 9 percent of those surveyed said the coastal plain of the ANWR should not be opened to oil and gas exploration. Most of the town's residents are standing beside the landing strip with open arms.

Another supporter of ANWR oil exploration is George Nasuayaaq Ahmaogak, mayor of the North Slope Borough, which encompasses nearly 90,000 square miles of Arctic territory at the top of Alaska. In a speech at the Arctic Power Annual Meeting on November 15, 2000, George spoke in favor of responsible drilling. He summed up his talk with, "We know that ANWR holds resources that can be safely extracted without destruction to the ecosystem. And that, ladies and gentlemen, is the bottom line."

This irritates the environmentalists, who think they know what the residents of the North Slope need better than they themselves do. The thing to remember is that the anti-drilling crowd means well. They are honestly trying to save the ANWR from what they see as a serious threat.

Personally, I think the needs of 281 million Americans should come before the needs of 175,000 caribou, animals that will not, according to the people who are most familiar with them, be adversely affected by the drilling anyway.

Besides, should oil exploration in the ANWR be stopped, it won't matter much to most of us what shape the area is in. Gas prices will probably keep us from ever getting to see it ...

WAKE UP AND SMELL THE DECAPPUCCINO

As distasteful as the thought is, I guess the only thing for me to do is apologize. Everyone makes mistakes now and then, so it was only a matter of time before I finally made one myself. It won't happen again. It may not have even happened this time.

The mistake I'm referring to was in a recent column I wrote about the effects of oil exploration in the Arctic National Wildlife Refuge. I said that, since the Gwich'in Eskimo people, who actually live in the ANWR, will be the ones most affected if the area were opened

KENDAL HEMPHILL

up to drilling, they should decide whether it is allowed. And I said the rest of us should keep our mouths shut.

That was poor advice.

For those of you who have not seen a newspaper, read a magazine, or turned on a television or radio for the past several months, the story goes like this: there's a bunch of oil in the ground in Alaska. George W. Bush wants to allow it to be pumped out so we won't have to buy so much oil from foreign nations. Robert Redford, Leonardo DeCappuccino, and a bunch of others want the oil left where it is, because they think the area would be polluted and the animals disturbed by the drilling.

I still believe the people who live in the ANWR should be the ones to decide what goes on there, but I no longer think we should all keep our mouths shut about it. And the reason I've changed my mind is that the people who are opposed to the drilling aren't keeping their mouths shut. And some of them have very big mouths.

A small but vocal minority seems to be worried about a relatively few caribou which, in all truthfulness, will most likely not be affected at all if drilling is allowed in the ANWR. But then, exaggerating the threat is a useful tool for those who don't care a lot about accuracy.

The ANWR contains 19.8 million acres, and the area proposed for oil and gas exploration makes up only 1.5 million of those acres. You can't tell me that even if the animals normally live right smack in the middle of where the drilling would occur, they can't find a suit-

THE BUCK NEVER GOT HERE

able place to live in the other 18.3 million acres. With only 175,000 caribou to begin with, that gives them over 113 acres apiece. Few Americans own that much land, and these are animals. Herd animals. They like to be together.

And there's plenty of space available in Alaska, which encompasses 365 million acres, and is the most sparsely populated state in the union. Pardon me for being callous, but the caribou can scoot over and quit hogging the countryside. I don't think they have more right to our land than we do. They are, after all, only caribou.

And they don't have to go far, really, to get away from the drilling. Frank Brown, who lives in Alaska, wrote to Mason County News editor Gerry Gamel in September about this issue. Frank serves on a committee with George Ahmaogak, mayor of the North Slope Borough, who believes responsible drilling in the ANWR is a good idea, as do almost all of the other residents of the area. They need the jobs and other benefits that opening the area to drilling would bring.

Frank said, "I could show you numerous photos of caribou herds resting peacefully around drilling rigs! The population of the central herd of the slope has increased by fourfold since Prudhoe Bay started production in 1977. The same claims were made in the 70s, but the facts have shown otherwise."

So almost everyone on the bandwagon against the Big Bad Oil Wolf seems to be misrepresenting the facts. I'm prepared to be gregarious, give them the benefit of the doubt, and say they're not lying to you on purpose. It's entirely possible they're just misinformed. Their motto could be 'Ignorant But Loud.'

The problem is they are using their misinformation to generate support for their cause among gullible Americans. Which is why I should not have said we should all mind our own business. The caribou huggers are encouraging as many as they can reach to write letters to everyone from President Bush to Smoky the Bear to let them know that drilling in ANWR is a Bad Thing. Most of the people voicing their opinions don't know any more about the area in question than Robert Redford does, but they're writing the letters anyway. You may as well write one too.

Being an outdoorsperson who loves to hunt, fish, camp, and hike in the unspoiled wilderness areas of our nation, it would be easy for me to throw in with the anti-drilling crowd. The problem is, being someone with common sense, I can't justify making the entire nation pay more than necessary for a gallon of gas, refined from oil bought from America's enemies, just because some alarmists think a few caribou might be adversely affected.

Besides, this country's economy is based on free enterprise. Somewhere along the line, it became unpopular to make a profit, and anyone who is successful in business is suddenly a Bad Person. Of course, those Bad People are the ones who employ the rest of us.

So write a letter to someone in charge and tell them what you think. Your opinion is just as important as Robert Redford's. He is, after all, only an actor.

THE BUCK NEVER GOT HERE

The bottom line is that if some self-appointed experts can speak out against Big Oil because they think a few caribou might be inconvenienced, you can speak out to help the Gwich'in people get what they need—jobs, improved schools, indoor plumbing, and a better lifestyle.

Because every American should have a right to a flush toilet...

HOLIDAYS

WHAT DOES CHRISTMAS MEAN TO YOU?

To most people, Christmas is a special time when families come together to visit, overeat, and play traditional games such as "Forty-two." At least, that's what it is for my family.

One of my earliest recollections of Christmas involves Santa showing up at our house on Christmas Eve and coming through the front door. I remember asking my dad why Santa didn't come down the chimney, and he said it was because we didn't have one. I guess that probably would have satisfied me, especially since Santa had a large duffle bag full of toys, but then my brother pointed out that Santa's belly had corners.

KENDAL HEMPHILL

Four of them. He had evidently lost a lot of weight working overtime on the toys and had to use a cardboard box to fill out his suit.

After that night, I was suspicious. Not only because of the box in the suit, or the front door entry either. There were other indications that something was rotten at the North Pole.

For instance, every year for a long time I asked Santa for a BB gun. All my friends had BB guns, and none were very good at sharing. Any time any of us got together, whether we were at the track or the creek or wherever, everyone else brought their BB guns. They would all shoot at cans, and rocks, and each other, and all I could do was wait 'til one of them had to go to the bathroom and hope he'd let me take care of his gun while he was gone. The problem with this was that most of my friends had extremely large, strong bladders. So I needed a BB gun of my own.

If you've ever seen the movie *A Christmas Story*, you know pretty much what happened to me. In the movie, Ralphie, a boy about nine years old, wanted a BB gun for Christmas. But not just any BB gun. He wanted an official, Red Ryder, walnut stocked, carbine action, 200-shot, range model air rifle. With a compass in the stock. He spent all his time trying to figure out how to get his parents to give him one for Christmas.

The only difference between Ralphie and me is that he got that BB gun for Christmas, and I never did. My folks stuck to their belief, probably correct, that I would just shoot my eye out, and never let me have a gun until I was old enough to have a real one.

THE BUCK NEVER GOT HERE

Even though I never got the BB gun, I don't think I would have completely lost faith in the big guy, had he come a little closer to the mark with what he actually brought me. I mean, if you ask for a hammer and get a saw, you're at least in the same vicinity. A mistake of that kind is understandable. But when you ask for a BB gun and get socks and underwear, something is definitely amiss.

Of course, when you're a kid, you don't expect things to work out perfectly. Adults, on the other hand, have a hard time accepting that concept.

My dad, for instance, always expected the Christmas lights to all work. He had a string of the old screw-in kind he'd gotten during FDR's administration, and they never seemed to want to cooperate until he'd expended at least ten hours on them. When we got ready to put up the tree, he'd stretch them out in a row on the living room floor and plug them in, evidently expecting them to just miraculously start shining. They never did, and he always seemed surprised for some reason. Then he'd start taking them out and switching them and putting them back in, working feverishly, until finally one of them, upon being screwed into a socket, would blow out in a shower of sparks, and all the lights in the house would go out. Then he would have to find a flashlight and hunt through the kitchen drawers for a new fuse, which, often as not, had to be borrowed from a neighbor.

Once he got the lights to all more or less shine at once, they had to be arranged on the tree very carefully, since we always had a real cedar tree, which was generally short and round and resembled a bush more than a tree. The lights had to be arranged just right because they would get hot after a while, and if one of the bulbs was allowed to rest against a flammable part of the Christmas bush (which meant any part of it), the whole thing could go up in flames. We heard stories about that happening all the time, sort of like the "starving kids in China" stories. I never could understand why, if having lights on a tree was so dangerous, my folks went to so much trouble to bring a tree in the house and put lights on it.

So several times a day, my brother and I were told not to touch the tree in any way, shape, form, or fashion. This was not only because we could cause one of the lights to touch a flammable part of the tree, but because if we moved any of the bulbs or wires at all, the lights were liable to quit working again.

The closer Christmas came, and the drier the bush got, the more nervous my folks became. A week before the big day we were instructed not to walk heavily, or even breathe deeply, in the room where the tree was. By Christmas Eve, we couldn't even look directly at the tree.

Nowadays, most everyone uses artificial trees, which cuts down on house fires, but also takes some of the excitement out of the season. I kind of miss the old days. Just one more time I'd like to spend Christmas Eve wondering if there was, just maybe, a Red Ryder BB gun under the tree for me. And barring that, it would be nice to get to fight a good Christmas tree fire ...

Oh, well. Merry Christmas anyway ...

THE BUCK NEVER GOT HERE

THE TRADITIONAL CHRISTMAS CARCASS

Christmas. A time of love. A time of hope. A time of joy.

If you're like most Americans, Christmas is a time when you would love for some of your relatives to stay home instead of spending the holidays spilling food on your living room rug. It's a time of hope that they will leave before they've eaten everything in your house, including the wax fruit. And it's a time of special joy when your loved ones finally back out of your driveway, and you can stop spending your evenings carrying a plunger from one bathroom to another.

But most of all, Christmas is a time of traditions. These are habits we get into, often not knowing why we do them, other than that our parents did them. For instance, most people decorate their homes with lights during the holidays, but few remember how this tradition got started.

Ancient Europeans used to get together on December 21, the winter solstice, to make a lot of racket and wave torches around. They did this to ward off the evil spirits, which they believed to be running around loose, since the veil between this world and the next was parted on the longest night of the year. We now know that the ancient Europeans had the intelligence of thatch, but we still put up Christmas lights. We do this because it's a tradition, and because Walmart sells them for two bucks a string.

Another tradition we observe at Christmas is giving each other gifts, which stems from when the

93

ancient Europeans used to give their relatives food, money, and clothes to get them to go home. We still give each other gifts today, although often without the desired effect. Sometimes relatives decide to stay longer after we give them something, and this is why the gag gift was invented. In hopes of disgusting the kinfolks into leaving, early Americans would give them something no one could possibly want. The perfect gag gift was originally a ringtail carcass in a box, such as the one some of my classmates gave to my Spanish teacher, Mrs. Edwards, at Christmas in 1976.

Mrs. Edwards was not the most popular teacher at Mason High School, and when she set up a Christmas tree early in December, on a table by the radiator, the temptation was just too great for some of the guys in our class. After skinning some coons one day, a few of them (the guys, not the coons) decided to give Mrs. Edwards a gift she probably still remembers, wherever she is. By the time it was discovered, the Christmas Carcass had nearly everyone in school gagging, hence the gag gift.

But as nasty a gift as the Christmas Carcass was, it was nowhere near as effective as were the Minnesota Christmas Pants, in terms of total gag gift irritation.

It all started in 1965, when Larry Kunkel received a pair of moleskin pants from his mother for Christmas. He soon found they froze stiff when they got really cold, an undesirable trait in pants for someone who lives in Minnesota. So, rather than move to Florida, Larry boxed up the pants the next Christmas and gave them to his brother-in-law, Roy Collette.

THE BUCK NEVER GOT HERE

The problem was that Roy also lived in Minnesota, and he didn't want the pants either. So he wrapped them up and gave them back to Larry a year later.

Larry and Roy played pants ping-pong for several years, until one Christmas when Roy jammed the pants into a three-foot-by-one-inch pipe to give them to Larry. The game had officially begun. The two brothers-in-law started wrapping the pants in more and more difficult packages, evidently trying to see if they could keep the other from getting to them, thus ending the game.

After getting the pants out of the pipe, Larry mashed them into a seven-inch square wrapped with wire and gave them back to Roy the next year. Roy then nailed the pants up in a two-foot-square crate filled with rocks, banded it with steel, and gave it to Larry.

The next year Larry had the pants sealed inside a double-pane window with a twenty-year guarantee and gave them back to Roy, who broke the glass and wadded the pants into a five-inch coffee can and soldered it shut. Then he imbedded the can into a five-gallon bucket full of concrete, complete with reinforcing steel, and gave them back to Larry.

Larry then made a 225-pound ashtray from eight-inch steel casings and engraved Roy's name on the side. The pants were inside the ashtray, and Roy had to use a cutting torch to get them out.

A year later, Larry received the pants inside a 600-pound safe, decorated with red and green stripes and welded shut. The next Christmas, he gave Roy a green, three-foot cube that had once been a 1974 Gremlin. The note attached to the one-ton cube informed Roy that the pants were in the glove compartment.

Roy returned the pants the next year, 1982, inside a tire filled with three tons of concrete. The tire was eight feet tall and two feet wide. The note on the outside said, "Have a Goodyear."

In 1983, Larry gave the pants back to Roy inside a seventeen-and-a-half-foot, red rocket ship full of concrete that weighed 12,000 pounds. The rocket was five feet in diameter, had six-inch pipes on the outside running the length of the ship, and sat on a launch pad. There was a picture of the pants on top of the rocket, and inside were fifteen canisters full of concrete. The pants were in one of these.

It took Roy a while to find the pants, but in 1985, he gave them back to Larry inside a four-ton, concrete Rubik's Cube, which had been baked in a kiln and covered with 2,000 board feet of lumber.

Larry's Christmas present to Roy in 1986 was a station wagon full of 170 steel generators welded together. The pants were somewhere inside.

How Roy gave the pants to Larry in 1987 is unknown, but just before Christmas in 1988, a flatbed truck pulled up in front of Roy's house, and a crane unloaded the tank from a concrete truck, full of concrete. The pants were somewhere inside.

I hate to tell you this, but I don't know what's happened to the pants since then. All I know is that, if there's one gift I don't want this Christmas, it's a pair of pants ...

THE BUCK NEVER GOT HERE

NUTS ABOUT THE INDIANS

One of my favorite things about the Christmas holidays, besides the opportunity to spend a lot of money on toys that will last about fifteen minutes before they're broken, is that there are so many delicious things to eat. And my favorite holiday food is anything with pecans in it. The only bad thing about pecans is that someone has to pick them up, and someone has to peel them.

I recently went to visit some old friends in San Saba who have a pecan orchard containing approximately ten billion trees, and I learned how pecans are supposed to be harvested. The Bynums have "gone automated" in harvesting their pecans, which means that, instead of crawling around on the ground picking them up, they now crawl around on the ground underneath their machinery, fixing it, so it will pick up pecans for them. Obviously, this is a much better system.

San Saba County, as you are no doubt aware, is the Pecan Capital of San Saba County, and most of the rest of the world. The country there is very sandy, which is very handy for getting stuck in. It's also very conducive to growing pecan trees.

The first step in harvesting pecans in sandy country is to "flatten the ground." Really. David Bynum, who is a chaplain in the u.s. Navy, also happens to be a topnotch welder. And if you've never welded top notches, it's not easy, let me tell you.

David built a large "ground flattener" to use on their orchard. And when I say large, I mean large. This

KENDAL HEMPHILL

device consists of a twelve-foot section of pipe, four feet in diameter, with 1 1/8-inch thick walls. It weighs 5,000 pounds. David welded caps into the ends of this pipe, mounted it on a *big* shaft, and built a sort of trailer around it so it can be pulled behind a *huge* tractor, to flatten the ground. Altogether, the flattener weighs 9,000 pounds. It can be filled with water to make it even heavier. So if you want flat ground, this baby can get the job done.

Once the ground is flat, you're ready to shake the trees. The Bynums have a smaller tractor with a shaker on the back, which can be operated from the driver's seat. You just back the tractor up to a tree, engage the shaker (which is no more complicated than your average nuclear reactor), and shake the wadding out of the tree. It feels like being out in a hailstorm, with the pecans falling all over you, but it sure beats using thrashing poles.

Stephen Bynum, a Department of Public Safety sergeant in Lampasas County, usually operates the "picker," which is the next step in the harvest. The picker looks like the "old-fashioned, moss-covered, three-handled, family gredunza" the Cat in the Hat drives in the Dr. Seuss book. One whole side of this machine is full of gears, pulleys, belts, and chains, and it raises such a cloud of dust it's normally completely obscured. Stephen usually looks like Pig Pen from the Peanuts cartoon at the end of a day at the orchard.

For the first minute I drove the picker, I was sure the steering mechanism had become disconnected

THE BUCK NEVER GOT HERE

somehow. But it was fine, it's just that the deep sand makes vehicles respond sluggishly, like maybe tomorrow. The picker has a small wheel in the rear that steers it, and two small wheels in the front, and the driver has to plan his turns a few minutes ahead of time. You get used to it after a while, or so Stephen said. You'd think it would be easy to avoid the trees in an orchard, with all the space there is between them, but when you're half blind, driving a temperamental vehicle that responds a good while after you turn the steering wheel, the trees had better get out of the way.

When the hopper on the picker is full, the pecans are dumped into a big machine called a "cleaner," which is about the most misnamed machine I've ever been involved with. After working at the cleaner for a few minutes, under a blower that spewed dirt, leaves, sticks, and whatever else wasn't pecans, I was definitely "dirtier." The pecans go through a hopper and come out the other side of the cleaner onto a conveyor belt, and someone has to stand there and pick out all the rocks, sticks, and bad pecans that come through the cleaner.

I was helping Otto "Ot" Bynum, Stephen and David's dad, pick the trash off the conveyor belt, and everything was going fine, until Ot noticed something that needed doing elsewhere and left me alone at the belt. Sometimes a whole bunch of bad pecans come through the cleaner at once, which is what happened while I was there alone. One minute, everything was fine, and I was happily picking out a pecan here and there, and all of a sudden there were twice as many bad ones, then three times, and

99

then four times as many. If you ever saw the classic *I Love Lucy* episode where Lucy got a job at the candy factory, wrapping the little chocolates as they came by on the conveyor belt, you know exactly what I looked like trying to run the cleaner by myself. There was no way to keep up, and I was hopping around like a one-legged dog trying to bury a bone on a frozen sand pile.

The conveyor belt dumps the pecans into a sack, which is then sewn up and taken to a pecan house and sold. While we were sewing sacks up, I asked about the different varieties of pecans, and the Bynums told me a bunch of facts I can't remember anything about, except that they were good facts.

The names of the different kinds of pecans impressed me quite a bit. They all seem to be named after Indians. There are Choctaws, Kiowas, Wichitas, Lamborghinis, Grubensteins, Lampshades, Armoirs, the list goes on and on. I said, "Ot, what'd they do, name all the pecans after Indians?"

Ot said, "Yep."

Ot is a man of few words.

I said, "Why'd they do that?"

Ot said, "I don't know."

So there you have it, the right way to harvest pecans. The next time you bite into a piece of fudge, or praline, or divinity, or pecan pie, think of me, and the trouble I went to to give you the facts, more or less, about pecan picking. And if you ever have the opportunity to help someone at their pecan orchard, just make sure you don't fall off the tractor and get run over by the flattener...

THE BUCK NEVER GOT HERE

INTERCEPTED LETTER TO SANTA

People for the Ethical Treatment of Animals
501 Front St.
Norfolk, Virginia 23510
Mr. Santa Claus
1 North Pole
Arctic Circle

Dear Mr. Claus,

Some time back, our organization was alerted to the possibility that you may be keeping wild animals captive, and we decided to look into the matter. What we have found is very disturbing.

Our investigation revealed that you do, in fact, have nine reindeer enslaved on your property at the North Pole. Reindeer, as you probably know, are classified as wild animals and are protected under the endangered species act (or should be, anyway). It is against the law for you even to have these animals in your possession, but your behavior and conduct toward these deer is even worse.

Our investigators found that you force these reindeer to live out-of-doors year round, even in temperatures in excess of forty below zero, and that they have to forage for food by raking snow and ice from the ground in order to get to the grass underneath. We are aware that reindeer commonly do this in the wild, but when kept captive, they should be fed and kept warm.

We also found that, once a year, you hook these peaceful creatures, who never harmed anyone, up to an enormous sleigh and make them pull it all over the world. This would be bad enough, but you actually ride in the sleigh and load it with a huge bag of contraband that you distribute to your constituents at every corner of the globe. The combined weight of the sleigh, bag, and yourself is clearly far more than these animals should be made to pull, especially since you are extremely obese. You're not even content with making them drag the vehicle on the ground, but force them to fly through the air pulling it. Please don't attempt to deny these charges, Mr. Claus, as we have actual videotape of your reprehensible actions.

We are aware that since these reindeer live outside, they could leave at any time. We know they stay with you and do your bidding of their own free will, but this has obviously been brought about through some type of subterfuge on your part, as reindeer in the wild do not, as a general rule, pull sleighs. We also hold that, being animals, reindeer do not know what is best for them, and that it is our job to see that their rights, as fellow beings on the planet we share, are respected.

Our investigators also found that you wear a suit trimmed with white, fuzzy material. This,

THE BUCK NEVER GOT HERE

we have decided, is obviously the fur of some animal, most likely the white arctic fox, which is also a protected species (or should be, anyway). In addition, your suit features boots and a wide belt, which are probably made from leather. We believe that, as a public figure, you should make an effort to set a better example for others and not wear the skins of animals on your body.

Since you see no harm in wearing leather and fur and live in a very cold climate, we have concluded that you are also, most likely, carnivorous. No doubt you subscribe to the ridiculous belief that eating the flesh and fat of animals helps to insulate the human body from the ravages of extremely cold weather. Nothing could be further from the truth. A steady diet of tofu would be just as beneficial to you.

We are aware, Mr. Claus, of your universal (and in our opinion, undeserved) reputation as a generous friend to children everywhere. Because of your lavish distribution of gifts to impressionable youths, you have managed to ingratiate yourself to the public at large. In light of this fact, we have decided to give you an opportunity to voluntarily redeem yourself.

We have decided that, in order to set things right, you will need to do the following:

1. Turn your illegally held reindeer over to peta and promise never to keep a wild animal captive again.

2. Publicly burn the well-publicized suit you are known for wearing, as a statement that people should not wear the skins and furs of animals.

3. Engage in not less than one hundred hours of community service, including marching in demonstrations protesting hunting, fishing, etc.

4. Buy a helicopter or airplane, so that in the future you will be able to deliver your gifts without having to enlist the aid of helpless animals.

Mr. Claus, if you choose not to cooperate with us in this matter, we will be forced to take legal action against you. We will expect a favorable response within thirty days.

For the record, our investigators also reported that you operate a sweatshop full of elves, requiring them to build your toys and trinkets for minimal pay, and setting terribly high quotas for them to meet. Since these elves, according to our research, are considered nearer to being human than animal, we have no interest in their welfare. However, rest assured that should you fail to comply with our demands, we will alert the proper authorities to your entire sordid operation.

Have an animal friendly day.

Sincerely,

Ingrid Newkirk

People for the Ethical Treatment of Animals

P. S. - We understand you will be making your regularly scheduled stops in Norfolk this Christmas Eve. This being the case, we would appreciate it if you would drop us off several cases of spray paint, as we plan to hit the fur and leather goods sections of some local department stores in the near future...

BE THANKFUL YOU'RE NOT A TURKEY

Thanksgiving is one of the few truly American holidays we have, a holiday that embodies the spirit that has made our nation the number one industrialized country in the world, in terms of total body fat per citizen. No other nation, that I can think of offhand, has a holiday requiring its participants to eat until they're legally unable to operate a motor vehicle, due to not being able to get the seatbelt fastened.

As you prepare for this year's Thanksgiving feast, I feel obligated to remind you of the words of Tarzan, which I remember from an old movie I saw when I was eleven. Tarzan was being tested by some African king,

KENDAL HEMPHILL

and he had to answer this question, "If you should meet an enemy after a thousand-mile journey, what is the one thing you would hope for?" Tarzan, being the star of the show, answered correctly. He said, "I would hope that it was he who made the journey."

That story obviously has nothing to do with Thanksgiving, except that when I sit down this November 26 to eat a meal that took ninety-three woman hours to prepare, most of it in a kitchen with men walking through demanding to know where the onion dip is (right now, before the commercial is over), the one thing I will hope for is that I wasn't the one who had to do all the cooking.

Of course, being a man, I don't have to worry about that. I can't cook anything more complicated than iced tea, and I can't even manage that unless the tea is already in a pitcher in the refrigerator. My wife would not ask me to prepare a meal unless she was in a total body cast and we had already eaten all the Pop-Tarts and cereal and potato chips and coasters in the house, and even then, she would wait until the children were showing definite signs of starvation.

Most men, I'm convinced, aren't any better at cooking than I am. Which is why, at Thanksgiving, there is a time-honored division of responsibility between the genders. The women are responsible for cooking the turkey, beans, and stuffing, baking the bread, pies, and cookies, tossing the salad, making the cranberry sauce, setting the table, pouring the tea, and calling "dinner's ready."

THE BUCK NEVER GOT HERE

The men are responsible for watching football on TV.

At least, that's the way we handle things in my family. If your family does things differently, fine. This is America, after all, and men are allowed to do things like cry and wear aprons. And if the men in your family want to fiddle with the balance of nature and help prepare Thanksgiving dinner, that's your business. Just as long as you don't tell the women in my family about it.

So the men pretty well have it made at Thanksgiving. The only real work they ever have to do is to carry a few chairs and set up a couple of card tables, and these jobs can be accomplished during halftime, with enough time left over to go to the bathroom and open a fresh bag of chips. This is great if you're a man, but if you're a woman, you'll want to remember what Tarzan said, and try to avoid having a bunch of folks come to your house on Thanksgiving, expecting you to feed them a thousand miles of turkey.

This is especially true if you happen to be the type of woman who feels the need to decorate your home to reflect the season. My wife is one of those, and when we have company during Thanksgiving she always goes to a lot of trouble to redo the house in a style I would call "Punitive Puritan." All the napkins and paper plates have to have turkeys or Quakers on them, and she drags in a pumpkin and some other inedible agricultural products and piles them in the middle of the dining room table. The purpose of this, I suppose, is to cause our guests to lose their appetites so she won't have to prepare as much food. I've managed, over the last several years, to get her to stop making everyone wear those silly, black, conical hats with the buckles on them, but I have to admit the stocks come in handy when the kids get too rowdy.

Every year, during the first part of November, the women in my family decide whose house to have Thanksgiving dinner at. I have no idea how this decision is made, and I don't want to know. It's possible they draw straws, or flip a coin, or play five-card stud, and the loser has to host everyone else. The men are told where to go and what time to be there. All they're concerned with, anyway, is how big the television screen is at the chosen house.

Since you women are the ones who have to do all the work, you should try to come up with some excuses as to why the event should be held somewhere besides at your house next year. A man can, with a clear conscience and without offending another man, say, "I don't want to have it at my house. I want to have it at your house so the kids can spill ketchup on your couch instead of mine." Women, for some reason, can't say things like that, even though they're thinking them.

Women are much more subtle, by which I mean vague. A woman would never come right out and say, "No, we're not going to have Thanksgiving dinner at my house, because Aunt Gladys always brings her disgusting poodle, and last year she threw up roach parts all over my rug. The poodle, not Aunt Gladys."

What you women should do is drop little hints throughout the year that will discourage your relatives from wanting to come to your house to eat. Whenever you can work them into the conversation, you should say things like, "Did you ever notice how much 'Mighty Dog' tastes like turkey?"

If it's too late for this year and you're having to host your family this Thanksgiving, good luck. Just remember that if your guests eat too much turkey and can't fasten their seatbelts, you are legally obligated to let them watch your television until the swelling goes down ...

THE TRUE MEANING OF CHRISTMAS

Now that Santa has retreated to the North Pole, the torn wrapping paper has been hauled off in a trailer, and most of the toys have been broken and the batteries run down, it's time to reflect on the true meaning of Christmas.

It's not the gifts. The kids get a big kick out of attacking the pile of brightly wrapped packages under the tree, but *they* still get something for nothing this time of year. That never happens to adults unless they're on welfare. It's enjoyable to watch the children open their presents, but it's more enjoyable to watch the relatives go home and stop sitting in the barcalounger hogging the remote control. So some would argue that the true meaning of Christmas is waving good-bye to the people who caused the septic system to back up.

But that's not it either. The true meaning of Christmas, for adults, is getting together with family and friends, being thankful for the relationships we have with one another, and eating enough traditional holiday food apiece to keep the average third-world citizen belching until long after the Clinton-Lewinsky scandal has been forgotten.

At Thanksgiving, your family probably sat down to a feast featuring a turkey the size of a Yugo station wagon (and possibly almost as dry), plus enough trimmings to founder a horse. For two weeks thereafter you had turkey sandwiches, turkey casserole, turkey soup, turkey pudding, turkey salad, etc., until you just about turned green if someone said "gobble." Eating turkey for Thanksgiving dinner, and turkey leftovers afterward, is as American as apple pie, which you probably had for dessert. And Christmas dinner is basically a rerun of Thanksgiving, except for a possible substitution of ham or roast for the entree.

Fact is, three hundred million turkeys are killed in the United States every year, forty million of them at Thanksgiving alone. I didn't just make these figures up out of a clear blue sky. I waited until after dark and made them up (Actually, I got them from peta's website). There are evidently a lot of people who are upset about all the turkeys who give their lives so you can get fed up, so to speak, with eating turkey. Fortunately, these people have offered a solution—tofu.

No doubt you're going to think I made this up, but I promise I did not. I have in front of me a copy of an article I got from peta's website (www.peta-online.org) entitled, "Have an Animal-Friendly Holiday Feast," which offers tofu as an alternative to turkey meat.

The article states, and I quote, "Two amazing meat-free 'turkeys' make holiday dinners a breeze. Tofurky (888-TOFURKY) and UnTurkey both include a savory soy-based roast, stuffing, and gravy. Tofurky even has 'dark-meat drumettes.'"

Due to my ignorance in the area of tofu, I decided to conduct some research and find out what it is. My research consisted of asking my wife, "What's tofu?" She said it was some stuff made out of soybeans. I asked her if it tasted like turkey, and she said it didn't, but that it contained a lot of protein.

The article also includes a recipe for "roast seitan," which calls for a "one pound piece of raw, unpoached seitan, half a pound of ground poached seitan, and one and a half cups of Basic Brown Sauce." I checked the current *Outdoor Annual*, TPWD's Hunting Regulations, and seitan is apparently not a game animal. At least there's not a season for it. When I asked my research department about seitan, she said she had no idea what it was, so if anyone out there knows what seitan is, I'd love to hear from you. I don't think I want to know what's in 'Basic Brown Sauce.'

The PETA website also contains a section called "Cooking With PETA," which offers many recipes for meat-free meals, including Vegetarian Sushi, Chicken Out! Nuggets with Maple-Mustard Dipping Sauce, Meat-free Chili, Shepard's Pie, Fajitas, and Burritos. None of these recipes sounds the least bit appetizing to me, but you may want to check out the site, in case PETA manages to talk Congress into an excise tax on meat, which is also proposed on their website.

The 'Tax Meat' article states that "America's meat-based diet costs this country billions of dollars in health care costs and billions more in environmental destruction. It's time for an excise tax on meat." According to peta, people who eat meat are at least 30 percent more likely to die of a heart attack, 40 percent more likely to get cancer, and at increased risk for many other diseases and illnesses, including stroke, obesity, appendicitis, osteoporosis, arthritis, diabetes, and food poisoning. The article also claims "Raising animals for food causes more detriment to human health and destruction of the environment than any other u.s. industry."

After having my personal eating habits attacked in this manner, I thought it was interesting that I got an email message from my friend, Charles Elbel, concerning bread. It seems a recent *Cincinnati Enquirer* headline read, "Smell of Baked Bread May Be Health Hazard." The article said that, among other dangers, the organic components of this aroma may break down ozone.

Charles doesn't remember who sent him the original message about this, but whoever it was claims to have done some research about bread and come up with some interesting statistics, which include:

- More than 98 percent of convicted felons are bread users.

THE BUCK NEVER GOT HERE

- Fully half of all children who grow up in bread-consuming households score below average on standardized tests.
- More than 90 percent of violent crimes are committed within 24 hours of eating bread.
- Bread is often a "gateway" food item, leading the user to "harder" substances such as butter, jelly, peanut butter, and even cold cuts. (Tofu is not mentioned, but draw your own conclusions.)
- Newborn babies can choke on bread.

The researcher suggests some restrictions on bread sales to help combat this problem, including prohibiting the sale of bread to minors, establishing "bread-free" zones around schools and, most ironically, a 300 percent federal excise tax on all bread sales, to help offset the costs bread imposes on society.

So it seems there are two sides to every story. Personally, I plan to keep destroying the environment and risking deadly diseases by sticking to my dangerous meat-based diet. Matter of fact, I think I'll throw caution to the wind and go make a batch of fudge... just as soon as I get my sewer line unclogged...

KIDS

VACATIONING IN COLORADO IS THE BEARIES

When I was a kid, my friends and I used to sing a song, adapted from the popular television series, about Daniel Boone being a man, a *big* man, but the bear being bigger and Daniel escaping up a tree. This song kept running through my mind recently, as I filled out the necessary forms to enable my eight-year-old son, Courtland, and I to go on an overnight backpacking trip in Rocky Mountain National Park. There are bears in the park.

My wife and I had decided to do Colorado the easy way, in a Jayco motor home. If you've ever gone on a long trip with young children, you know that traveling by burro train across Siberia without kids would be more enjoyable than driving a couple of hours in a luxury limousine with three bored youngsters.

My three kids probably get along about as well as any siblings, which means they can tolerate each other for a while as long as all of them are asleep in different states. After five minutes in the back of our van, they're usually unable to breathe without punching each other, and they seem to believe that death would be preferable to giving up half an inch of 'their' space. And no matter how many toys each of them has, they all *always* want to play with the same thing at the same time. So we got a twenty-six-foot Jayco Eagle motor home, loaded up the kids and everything else we could cram into it, and took off for the mountains.

I must admit I was a little apprehensive about driving such a large vehicle into unfamiliar country, but the Jayco turned out to be no more difficult to drive down the street than your average-sized Walmart store. (Actually, once you get used to it, a motor home is no problem to drive at all. You just have to remember not to try to pull into Sonic.)

One of the main advantages to driving a house on vacation is convenience. For one thing, it isn't necessary to lug your luggage into and out of motel rooms every day, with the ensuing, "Have you looked under the bed and in all the drawers and in the bathroom to make sure we aren't leaving anything here? Well, look again, just to make sure."

THE BUCK NEVER GOT HERE

For another thing, reservations are usually not needed. We found out that a great many people who travel in motor homes spend a lot of their nights in the parking lots of twenty-four-hour Walmart stores. This, however, has a down side. If you think you spend too much money at Walmart now, try living in front of one for a week and a half.

But the most significant advantage to traveling in a motor home is that the kids aren't constantly breathing down Dad's neck with the usual complaints, such as "Are we there yet?" and "How much longer?" and "I'm hungry," and "I need to go to the bathroom," and of course, the dreaded, "Never mind, it's too late." In a motor home, the kids can eat, watch television, go to the bathroom, and break each other's toys, all while the family is still driving down the road.

Colorado turned out to be quite pleasant, despite being inhabited mostly by people from Colorado. To be honest, there are probably almost as many Texans in Colorado during the summer as there are foreigners. We even met a couple of Park Rangers at Rocky Mountain National Park, George and Cindy Smith, who are from Bulverde, Texas. They spend seven months during the summer in Colorado and the rest of the year in Texas. Mrs. Smith was helpful in a lot of ways, not the least of which was making us feel at home.

We spent a few days in the Manitou Springs area being typical tourists. We spent half a day at the Garden of the Gods, a 1,300-acre park donated to the city of Colorado Springs under the stipulation that it would always remain free to the public. Visitors can explore the huge, red rocks in the park and, at the risk of a $500 fine, climb up on the rocks and fall to their deaths. Technical climbers are required to obtain a permit, thereby falling to their deaths without the risk of a fine.

We went to the Manitou Cliff Dwellings, where ancient Indians lived in ancient mud houses built into the side of an ancient mountain. Visitors are encouraged to go inside the houses and, to keep from bumping their heads on the low ancient ceilings, squat in the ancient dirt. The boys loved it.

We rode the Cog Railway to the top of Pike's Peak, where we hurriedly scurried inside the Summit House, since the temperature at 14,110 feet was forty-two degrees. We ate some doughnuts made from a special, high-altitude recipe, and seriously considered buying t-shirts that said, "Got Oxygen?" They seemed extremely appropriate at the time.

After a few days, we headed north and visited the Air Force Academy, and then went on up and spent a couple of nights in Estes Park, located on the eastern edge of Rocky Mountain National Park. We stayed a couple of nights in RNMP, which is where Courtland and I went backpacking. Bears are becoming a problem there, and before I was issued an overnight permit to camp out in the park, I was required to read and sign a form that stated that, should we be eaten by a bear, our family would not sue the pants off Uncle Sam.

We started off with high hopes, Courtland hoping we would see a bear, me hoping we wouldn't. We hiked ten miles to our campsite, took some pictures of some elk, which were conveniently located nearby, ate supper, and pitched our bivy tent for the night.

As we were packing up to hike out the next morning, I told Courtland that, as disappointing as it was, it looked like we wouldn't get to see a bear. Five minutes later, I looked up, and there was a huge black bear, bigger than a horse, ambling down the trail toward our camp. I hollered the most intelligent thing I could think of to say, "Courtland, there's a bear!" and dove for a camera (hoping to leave some evidence to tell rescuers what had happened to us) while Courtland grabbed his "bear stick." By the time I turned back around, the bear was ambling off through the trees. Courtland must have scared him off.

All things considered, it was a lovely trip, especially since we didn't become an entree for *ursus bigtoothus*. So if you're planning a vacation for next summer, I highly recommend a trip to Colorado. Remember what happened to Daniel and me, though, and try to spend most of your time in the motor home, or in Walmart...

BOYS AND BOWS–A DANGEROUS COMBINATION

I love kids. So does my wife. We love kids so much we have three of them ourselves, although, if there had been a trial program, we might not have gone quite so far overboard.

The way we ended up with three kids is, one day my wife said to me, she said, "Honey, we need more dirt in our lives." Also, I had noticed there were never any Cheerios in my boots. They just sat in my closet when I wasn't wearing them, an excellent place to store things like marbles and extra Cheerios so your brother couldn't find them, but they were always empty. So now we have three boys, and we no longer feel the need for more dirt, and the inside of my boots is no longer wasted space.

Now, being an archer, I'm teaching my boys to shoot bows, at least while they're not too busy picking their noses or trying to put bugs into each other's ears.

On his third birthday, my middle son, Paden, was given a little fiberglass bow and three suction-cup arrows. I spent several hours showing him how to shoot it, and then watched as he drew the bow and shot an arrow backwards over his right shoulder. I decided we needed to spend a little more time on which direction the arrow should go. At least he let go of the *string* and not the *bow*. We're making progress.

At that time my youngest son, Leret, was only seven months old, and wasn't into archery much yet, although I gave him an old shooting glove. He immediately showed his appreciation by seeing if he could get it all into his mouth at once and covering it with an impressive layer of drool.

Courtland, then five, was a fine archer. With a twenty-pound bow and my old arrows, he could easily scare the wadding out of any cat stupid enough to wander within his range, which he claims is forty miles but is closer to eight feet.

THE BUCK NEVER GOT HERE

One day, my wife was throwing twelve-inch disks up for me to shoot at (and miss), and Courtland wanted to shoot at one. I lined him up and got him all ready, and when I pitched up a disk, he drilled it. First shot. Dead center. I can't describe the feeling that came over me. I was so proud of him I could have wrung his little neck, but I refrained because my wife was watching. He wanted to shoot at some more disks, but I carefully explained to him that it was illegal for someone under twelve to hit the first disk he shot at, but if he wouldn't shoot any more, I'd keep my mouth shut.

Near Mason, Texas, where we live, feral hogs range freely, and recently a sow and six small pigs decided to freely range into our backyard to sleep every night. This sow was rather picky about having fresh linens, and she rooted herself and her pigs a new wallow daily. Our yard soon looked like the French countryside in an old WW II movie. Every morning I expected to look out the window and see Ronald Reagan leading an ethnically varied squad of u.s. soldiers in a desperate attack on our back porch.

I decided the pigs were old enough to either get jobs or go on welfare, so it was time to get rid of the sow and save the yard. I was loading my quiver, getting ready to go after her, when Courtland came in, watched me for a minute, and said, "I want a broadhead."

I looked at my son carefully for a moment and said, "Son, get your finger out of your nose." And I meant it.

"I want a broadhead," he repeated. The time had come to make a decision. I thought about what I should do, squared my shoulders, and made up my mind. I squatted down, looked him right in the eye, and said, "Go ask your mother."

He didn't like that idea a whole lot, and protested on the grounds that his mother never let him do anything fun, by which he meant life-threatening. Kids, especially boys, spend most of their time trying to kill each other, except when they're alone, and then they try to kill themselves.

He knows he's got a better shot with me. I'm a pushover. I always let him do dangerous stuff like get on the roof with me when I have to clean out the gutters or something, and I always make him promise not to tell his mother, which is the first thing he does when he sees her.

Anyway, my kids aren't the only ones learning archery. A while back, I shot with Bobby Buff, founder of "Traditional Bowhunters of Texas," at a traditional archery tournament at Fredericksburg, Texas, and his son, Zachary, shot with us. Zach was almost six, and had a very laid back attitude toward archery. Often, when his dad was at full draw and the rest of us were trying to be fairly quiet, Zach would look up from poking in the dirt with his bow tip and say, "Hurry up and shoot, Dad." Did wonders for Bobby's concentration.

Even with all that help, early in the shoot Bobby shot a deer target in the leg, about knee height. Zach was very encouraging and tried to make Bobby feel better. "Dad," he said, "that was about the worst shot I ever saw." This is the kind of warm, friendly camaraderie I hope to have with my boys one day.

If you're thinking about having children, I highly recommend girls ...

KIDS–OUR HOPE FOR A
BRIGHTER TOMORROW

If you are a concerned, caring outdoorsperson, as I am, then the most important thing you can do to help ensure that future generations of Americans will be able to enjoy the outdoors is to take your kids hunting, fishing, and camping with you as often as possible. This is also the easiest way I know to become a permanent resident of the nearest state mental institution.

My wife and I take our kids into the outdoors as often as possible, and not just to keep them from spending all their time doing permanent damage to our house. No, the main reason we get out a lot is that our youngest, Leret, is not yet potty trained, and the outdoors usually smells better than our indoors.

We were getting ready to go to the river recently for a cookout, and my five-year-old, Paden, asked me if I was taking my fly fishing rod. When I told him I was he said, "Good, 'cause I really want to see what a flyfish looks like."

The kids had been playing in the river for a while when Paden came running over to me, crying, holding his knee. I asked him what was wrong and he said, "I fell and hurt my knee on those dam rocks."

I said, "WHAT DID YOU SAY?" I spoke in capital letters to show the depth of my concern about the language he was using. I was wondering if maybe he'd been hanging out at a pool hall or something.

He said, "I hurt my knee on those dam rocks over there." He pointed to a dam he and his brothers had been building in the shallow water, and I finally figured out that, when he said "dam rocks," he was referring to the rocks in the dam.

Leret, being a normal three-year-old, has a lot of trouble just walking around on a flat floor, so naturally he tries to climb every tree he sees. Three-year-old boys have an instinctive desire to damage themselves in the most expensive ways they can think of, in terms of emergency room costs.

This need to hurt themselves hits children at different ages, depending on the individual child. We had a cookout at the river once with some friends who had a five-year-old daughter named Julie who, during the course of the evening, tripped over the exact same piece of driftwood at least forty times. Her parents finally bought her a bicycle helmet and made her wear it all the time, in an effort to keep from being reported to the authorities for child abuse because of her injuries.

My oldest, Courtland, is seven, and has a friend named Dakota. Dakota spent an afternoon at our house swimming with the kids in their kiddy pool a while back, and several hours later reported that he had lost a tooth. When my wife, Jocelynn, asked him where it was he said, "I don't know. I lost it in the pool." Jocelynn later found the tooth and gave it to Courtland to return to Dakota.

The next day, Courtland asked her if the Tooth Fairy looked in your mouth when she came to leave money for a lost tooth. Jocelynn asked him why he wanted to know, and he wouldn't answer. She finally

THE BUCK NEVER GOT HERE

got him to admit that he was planning to leave Dakota's tooth under his pillow that night and try to cash in on it himself.

Last January, Paden and Leret went with me to sell some coons I had killed. Paden wanted to know what was going to happen to the coons, and I told him their hides would be tanned and made into furs. He asked if he could have their teeth, and I managed to squeeze out of him that he was planning to try to outwit the Tooth Fairy the same way Courtland had wanted to with Dakota's tooth, but he wanted to use coon teeth instead of human ones. I could almost see the dollar signs in his eyes when he saw how many teeth the coons had.

Taking kids hunting is always a lot of fun, right up to the point where you actually leave the house. I've found that deer hunting with kids is usually a mistake until they reach at least age six. Kids younger than that have a very hard time sitting still and being quiet, unless they can run around and make a lot of noise while they're doing it.

Dove hunting is a good way to introduce children to the outdoors, since it involves a lot more latitude in the areas of movement and noise than deer hunting. Kids also come in handy for fetching downed birds.

When a friend of mine took his four-year-old son, James, dove hunting for the first time, the boy was fascinated by the way a dove would flop around after its head had been pulled off. Once, while he was watching this take place, James looked up at me and said, "He can still flap his wings; he just can't see."

There is really no substitute for the experiences a child can gain from outdoor activities. Besides giving them a chance to learn about the world they live in, being outside keeps kids from vegetating in front of the television, which scientists now believe causes cancer in laboratory rats.

Groups such as Operation Orphans, the Texas Youth Hunting Association, and ROE (Responsible Outdoor Education) are working to educate America's children and get them into the woods to hunt, and all these groups need your help and support. Giving kids a chance to go hunting when they would otherwise never have the opportunity is a gift that will last a lifetime.

Of course, to some kids, such as those who grow up in most of Texas, hunting comes naturally. I was explaining Groundhog Day to my boys a couple of years ago, and when I had told them what happened if the groundhog saw his shadow and what happened if he didn't, Courtland thought for a minute and then asked, "What happens if you shoot him?"

BOATING

TIPPYCANOE AND NINTENDO TOO

Now that spring has sprung, the weather is beautiful outside, and school has let out for the summer, you're probably thinking about getting out and doing some outdoor type stuff. Maybe you're trying to come up with an activity that will help pry your child away from the Nintendo game for a while, and give him the self-confidence necessary to become a productive member of society, or at least not end up a used car salesman or a politician. If so, maybe you should consider canoeing.

For many centuries, man has been going forth and becoming acquainted with the natural waterways of natural nature in a very personal way through canoeing. For many centuries, man has also been turning his canoe over and getting naturally dunked in these natural waterways. It's a little known fact that this is how bathing and swimming were invented to begin with. Unfortunately, so was drowning.

Early boaters used their craft for a variety of purposes, such as fishing, hunting, portaging, recreation, and turning over in the rapids. This is where a lot of today's ancient artifacts came from. Scuba divers recently discovered, buried under several feet of silt on the bottom of the Nile River in Germany, a 1,500-year-old pair of Ray Ban shades.

The first canoes were, naturally, nowhere near as advanced as the ones available today. They were basically sectors of trees, ten to forty feet long, split in half, and hollowed out with sharp rocks. They were known as 'we-no-na,' from the ancient Greek words *we* meaning "don't," and *no-na* meaning "rock the boat."

Despite being crude and heavy, early canoes showed a lot of the potential that has been realized in their more modern cousins. After many hours, days, weeks, months, and years of hard work, shaping and smoothing the wood to just the right thickness and form, one can imagine the pride these early mariners felt as they slid their finished boats into the water and watched them gurgle gracefully to the bottom. "Maybe," the early mariners said to each other while scratching their heads, "we shouldn't have used petrified wood."

Later, canoes were made from birch bark, hunks of which were stripped from the trunks of Aspen trees

THE BUCK NEVER GOT HERE

and sewn together on early Singer sewing machines, then stretched over a framework of PVC pipe. These canoes were a vast improvement over their predecessors, being much lighter in weight, and often didn't sink until someone actually boarded them. Then boat builders learned to caulk up the cracks between the strips of bark with "pitch," an early form of epoxy, and people could finally actually ride in the canoes.

Today's outdoorsperson has a few more options than these boating pioneers. There is a wide variety of canoes available for purchase commercially, ranging in price from $300 to several thousand simoleans (a French term meaning either "pesos" or "don't rock the boat").

If you'd like to try canoeing but aren't sure you'll like it, and you don't want to spend a lot of money to find out, you would do well to rent a boat a few times before you buy one. A canoe rental business is also a good source if you're interested in buying a used canoe at a reasonable price. They always have some boats they're willing to sell, and you can save a lot of money this way. The most reputable canoe rental business I'm aware of in Texas is the Rock Bottom Canoe Company, located in Mason. And I'm not promoting canoeing because I am the owner and proprietor of Rock Bottom Canoe Company and I want to rent or sell you a boat, although all that is true. I'm promoting canoeing because I have an inherent love for the outdoors and want to encourage you to get out and experience the joys of recreational boating as I have. So I can rent or sell you a boat.

If you do decide to try canoeing, there are a few things you should know going in. These things will probably not make your canoeing experience easier, or more fun, or less dangerous, but they will definitely help me come up with another three hundred or so words for this column, and I feel compelled to list these things for you, just as soon as I think them up.

OK, here's one—canoes, by and large (more by than large) would rather float down the river upside down than upside up. They will tip over and spill you at the slightest provocation. This is where the famous city "Tippycanoe," which is near Tyler, Texas, got its name. There is nothing you can do about the tippyness of canoes, I just thought you should know.

Ha! I jest. Actually, there are a few precautions you can take to keep your canoe from dumping you in the water. One is to leave it on land. This is an especially advisable precaution, most especially advisable during the winter months, since water seems to be colder during those times. But staying on land makes paddling difficult.

Another precaution is to be a woman. I am not trying to be discriminatory here, but it is an actual fact that the higher the payload of a canoe is above the waterline, the less stable the canoe is. Another actual fact is that women have a lower center of gravity than do men. We will not go into *why* women have a lower center of gravity than men. I have probably already said too much, since I am married to a woman, and women also have a lower tolerance for insinuation than men. That's all I got to say about that.

Paddling also presents a problem for canoeists, even if they're female ones. You may notice from reading your Bible that prior to the Great Flood, God told Noah to build an Ark with one window, one door, and no paddles. There is a very good reason for this, besides the fact that the world would be covered with water, and Noah would have nowhere to go. God knew that if Noah and his family tried to paddle, they would turn the ark over, and you would not be here to read this column.

When canoeing, you should try to keep your weight in the center of the boat, but you have to lean out a little to paddle, and this causes you to flip. The answer, of course, is to use a very long paddle, so that after you flip you can extend it to someone on shore and they can pull you out.

Armed with this advice, I'm sure you'll spend many a happy hour on the water this summer. If you have any questions feel free to call me. I'll be at home, playing my children's Nintendo game...

BULL DURHAM-STYLE BOAT BUILDING

Judging from the comments I've heard lately, it seems a great many people are becoming interested in canoeing. This is a good thing. Canoeing is a healthy, wholesome, enjoyable outdoor activity the entire family can participate in for most of the year, or until such time as one or more members of the family drowns.

One of the main problems with getting started canoeing, however, is the cost of a high-quality boat.

New canoes are not exactly cheap, and finding a good, used canoe for sale can be difficult. For this reason, many aspiring mariners choose to build their own boat.

Of course, cost is not the only reason people build boats. My friend, Mike Innis, and his brother, George, built a fourteen-foot wooden sailboat recently, not because they couldn't afford to buy a boat, but so that Mike would have something to fill up his garage. They also claimed they were building the boat for the enjoyment of it but, having witnessed the builders at work on more than one occasion, I would have to question that motivation. They seemed to spend a lot of their time talking and scratching their heads, looking at boat plans, going to town for supplies, taking breaks, building forms and patterns, and getting something to drink, etc.

I have to admit, however, that when Mike and George finally finished their boat, I was impressed. It's a real beauty. Mike even claims they actually took it to a lake once to try it out, but I would have to question that too, since I have only seen it out of his garage once, when he pulled it around town on a trailer. It does look very nice in the garage, though.

The point I'm trying to make here is that you can build a boat yourself, with a minimum of expense and only rudimentary carpentry skills, as long as you have a brother named George.

The first item on the agenda when building a boat is to decide what you're going to use it for. If you plan to fish with a friend in small lakes and rivers, you'll probably want to build a canoe. If you'll be boating alone,

THE BUCK NEVER GOT HERE

you might rather have a small kayak. If you intend to sail around the world, you'll most likely want to build a slightly larger boat. Wear a life jacket.

Once you figure out what kind of boat you want to build, you'll have to decide whether you want to come up with your own design, or buy a set of plans to follow. I suggest buying plans, since I've built a canoe by my own design, and the result was somewhat less than satisfactory.

What happened was I wanted a canoe, and my wife didn't want me to buy one. Something about needing the money for food or some such. Anyway, I had an old, steel pressure tank, and I decided to build a canoe out of it.

I cut the bottom off, just above where it curved in, with a saber saw. Then I cut it half in two, lengthwise, butted the two halves together, and welded up the seam. I used a sledgehammer to bang the ends into a sort of pointy shape, and slapped a couple of boards across the gunwales for seats. It wasn't beautiful, or elegant, or stable, or lightweight, or comfortable, but the one thing my canoe was was tough. With an eighth-inch steel hull under me, I definitely did not have to worry about hitting a rock and damaging my boat.

If you decide to go with someone else's plans, you'll have an almost infinite number of choices to pick from. Volumes have been written about homemade boats. Look in the back of any fishing, canoeing, or outdoor magazine and you can find ads offering everything from plans for individual canoes to books containing the plans for lots of different boats.

One such book, *Instant Boats,* was written by Harold "Dynamite" Payson. It mostly contains plans for building sailboats, which I am not interested in, but I included it here because I like to write Harold 'Dynamite' Payson.

I borrowed *Instant Boats* from my friend, Bob McRee, who is the preacher at the Mason Church of Christ and an experienced boat builder. Bob has built at least two actual, wooden boats, and is considering building another one. I thought that sounded pretty impressive, until Bob showed me the plans for his next boat.

It's called the Six-Hour Canoe, due to the fact that someone with virtually no woodworking skills whatever can, by carefully following the plans, build one in three months.

Not really! You can build one in about six hours, according to Dick Butz, who wrote an article about this boat in the August 1995 issue of *WoodenBoat Magazine.* Dick claims that kids as young as eleven have successfully constructed the Six-Hour Canoe, which only requires two sheets of thin plywood, some scrap lumber, a bottle of glue, and some fairy dust.

Another friend of mine, Terry Peavy of Voca, Texas, is a master craftsman and has built at least one canoe and one Aleut kayak, both of which are the "wooden-framework-covered-with-canvas" type. Terry loaned me the plans for the kayak, and I made a copy of them, but I seriously doubt I will ever attempt to build one. Besides being approximately the size of the Dallas/Ft. Worth phonebook, the Aleut kayak plans include terms

THE BUCK NEVER GOT HERE

such as *gusset, chine,* and *spar,* which, quite frankly, I would rather not have to go to the trouble to learn.

Whichever type of boat you decide to build, one thing is certain—you won't learn how to build it from this column. But with a healthy dose of determination, a lot of elbow grease, your wife's grocery money, and a little luck, you can have greasy elbows in no time. Then you can call your brother, George, and get him to build you a boat...

CAMPING

A RIVER RUNS OVER IT

After spending the Fourth of July camping on the river with my family and thirty or forty other people, I started wondering why we do the things we do for recreation. Camping has always been fun for me, but since acquiring a wife and three kids, it's a little more complicated than it used to be.

When I was in high school my friends and I (yes, I had friends, although no one else could see them) went camping fairly often. We never took a lot in the way of gear, since most of us didn't have much. But that was all right, since none of us had wives or kids. We had few requirements.

If a dozen of us went on an overnight trip to the river, we would each take a sleeping bag or blanket, a fishing rod, and a pocketknife. We would take an ice chest with our drinks and some weenies in it, and maybe a box or two of frozen bait shrimp. Our other groceries included a couple of packages of hot dog buns, a can of Wolf brand chili, several bags of potato chips, and some Chips Ahoy! cookies. That was about it.

Camping with my wife and three boys is very similar to moving. For our Independence Day river trip, we took a Dodge Grand Caravan loaded to capacity with stuff, a Chevy pickup equally encumbered, and a trailer containing two canoes and four kayaks. We spent less than twenty-four hours at the river.

Now, I'm not complaining, you understand, but I want to make it clear that I don't believe all that stuff was necessary. Not that I mind having some extra clothes and maybe a roll of toilet paper along 'just in case,' but we took more gear with us for an overnight camping trip than General Patton's army took with them when they invaded France.

Of course, each of us had to have a bedroll and several sets of clean clothes, and we took a couple of Coleman lanterns. My wife took enough food for twenty people, including something from each major food group, including, but not limited to, the paper plate group, the napkin group, and the plastic utensil group.

We took several towels, swimsuits for everyone, a folding camp table, two folding chairs, three stools, a Formica tabletop and a pair of folding sawhorses, a

THE BUCK NEVER GOT HERE

Coleman compact two-burner gas camp stove, a two burner propane camp stove, a Coleman one-burner stove, styrene pool noodles for the kids, extra shoes for everyone, three bottles of sunscreen, a non-stick griddle, several skillets, plastic tablecloths, a roll of paper towels, two five-gallon bottles of propane, extra Coleman fuel, several aluminum plates, two shovels, half a cord of mesquite wood, a tent, a folding cot, scissors, four ice chests, and sixty pounds of ice. For one night at the river.

When I was a kid, we never needed all that stuff. Towels, for instance, were viewed as a luxury item more trouble than it was worth. Being wet was not seen as a problem. If we didn't want to be wet, we stayed out of the river.

Few of my friends had a Coleman stove or lantern when we were growing up. Anyone with one of those items was always welcome on any camping trip, even if no one liked them, but most of the time we had to do without. Sometimes we took flashlights, but the batteries usually quit or the bulbs burned out about thirty minutes after dark, and even if we had new batteries and bulbs, the lights we could afford weren't much use. I generally had to strike a match to see if my flashlight was on or not. When it got dark, we gathered driftwood, built a campfire, and cooked supper (hot dogs impaled on sharpened sticks and chili heated in its own can). If we had to venture very far from the fire, we did a lot of stumbling and falling and ended up wishing we'd brought some Band-Aids, or maybe a tourniquet or splint.

KENDAL HEMPHILL

Tables and chairs were totally unnecessary. We ate standing up, squatting, or sitting on the ground, and we held our food in our hands. We saw no point in putting a hot dog down, since we would just have to pick it up again to take the next bite, so we never used plates. We had no need of napkins either. If we got chili on our hands, we licked off what we could and wiped the rest on our shirts.

We never used tents or cots when I was a kid either. We generally rolled our sleeping bags or blankets out on the ground near our campfire and hoped a rattlesnake or water moccasin didn't decide to crawl in with us. Scorpions and centipedes were more likely, but no more welcome. We often woke up covered with ants, and mosquitoes were always a problem. If we didn't get snake bit, stung, or have all our blood siphoned out, we got rained on. A tent would have protected us from most of these hazards, but then it wouldn't have seemed like real camping.

We never took sunscreen either. Rubbing lotion on our exposed skin would have taken upwards of two or three minutes, which would have had to come out of our total allotment of river time. This was clearly unacceptable. Besides, total coverage was not an option. It's almost impossible to apply that stuff to the middle of your own back, and a teenage boy would rather eat a Zebco reel than ask another teenage boy to put lotion on him. We'd rather burn, which is what we did. Medium well, as I recall.

It generally took us a few days to recuperate from a river trip when I was in high school, due to the large amount of pain and suffering we inflicted on ourselves in the name of recreation. Now it's different. Now it takes me about a week to get back to normal. Not that the trip itself is all that taxing, but the loading and unloading wears me down to a nub. I don't know what's worse—hauling all that stuff to the river and back, or doing without it.

Sixty pounds of ice. I still can't believe it...

GEORGE WASHINGTON GOT RAINED ON HERE

On a recent bowhunting trip, I camped out two nights. Well, I didn't really camp out. What I really did was spend two nights sleeping in a trailer made out of a pickup bed with a camper shell on it. To many people, I realize, this would be "roughing it," the height of self-flagellation. To me it's cheating. To me, and to a great many other outdoorspersons, you're not really camping out unless you sleep on the ground or in a tent.

My first tent was a birthday present from my parents when I was about seven. It consisted of a six-by-eight-foot canvas tarp, several short ropes, and three wooden poles. It was called a "pup tent," evidently because when erected, only a puppy would fit inside with any comfort. And although it was small, my first tent had the advantage of weighing only sixty pounds, an ideal weight for camping trips thirty yards from home or less. Luckily, I never camped that far from the house.

The main attraction to having such a simple, basic tent was that it was so easy to set up. My dad showed me how to do it, and after only a few months of practice, I was able to drag it into the yard, tangle the ropes, bonk myself over the head with one of the poles, and lose Dad's hammer in only an hour and a half. To my recollection, I never managed to set that tent up alone. When I could talk Dad into setting it up for me, I would lie in it for hours, staring up at the "ridgepole" a couple of feet above my head, and pretend I was off in a wilderness somewhere, having an adventure. I even spent a few nights in that tent in the backyard, bravely camping out by myself, at least until it got dark.

That first tent had no floor and was open to the elements at both ends, features which would seem, at first glance, to be disadvantages. Not so. On the few occasions when I inhabited the tent during a backyard rain shower, I hardly noticed the rain blowing in the open ends, due to the fact that water was coming through the roof even faster. And a floor would only have slowed drainage.

Soon after my wife and I were married, we bought a "three-person dome tent" at JC Penny. This tent was evidently named by the foreman of a road construction crew. It soon became obvious that "three-person tent" meant that one person could sleep inside while two people stood outside and watched. It was a freestanding tent held up by fiberglass poles, and the first time we used it we neglected to stake it down. With nothing inside to give it weight, our new tent was picked up by a gust of wind and wafted away, bouncing merrily along through

THE BUCK NEVER GOT HERE

the weeds, brush, and brambles of the pasture we were camping in. We never would have caught up with it if it hadn't gotten hung up on a barbed wire fence.

Ripped, torn, gouged, and lacerated, we still used that tent whenever we went camping, until we started having children and needed more space. So my wife bought a "cabin tent'" at a garage sale for four dollars, sans directions, and happily brought it home for me to hate. Although I set that tent up numerous times on hunting and camping trips, I never, as far as I know, set it up right. It always sagged and sighed and seemed to look sort of bored. And it shed water like a colander.

The last time we used that four-dollar tent was when we attended the Big Flood of June '97, on the Frio River in Concan, Texas. Sunny when we set up camp, it started raining soon after dark. My wife and I and our three kids spent all night arguing over who was lying in the warmest puddle.

We've moved up a long way since then. Now we have an eight-by-twelve-foot Red Head tent from Bass Pro Shops. It is, by far, a much nicer tent than I ever imagined owning. It's lightweight, tough as a boot, easy to set up, and fits snugly into its own carrying bag. It keeps out rain and bugs, yet allows a breeze on warm nights. It's big enough so we can put the kids down for a nap in one end and entertain guests in the other. It's just the kind of tent the National Park Service should buy to replace George's.

I refer, of course, to a recent Associated Press article sent to me by several alert outdoorspeople, the headline of which reads "George Washington's tents in need of repair." The article states that some tents that belonged to the father of our country on display at the Park Service's visitor center at the Yorktown battlefield were damaged recently by a faulty air system, which blew some oily dirt onto them. They also received a large water stain, thanks to a leak in an air conditioner. The Park Service is now trying to raise a few bucks to put these tents back into top condition, or as near top condition as two-hundred-year-old tents can be put into. They don't need much, just $400,000.

Now, I can hear you cynics out there, saying it's stupid to spend that kind of cash on a couple of old tents, and that the National Park Service should have had cheap replicas made instead of putting the real McCoy in the visitor center, and that George isn't likely to need those tents again anytime soon, and that the founding fathers being novices at government, and not knowing how to spend money, the tents probably didn't cost more than $100,000 when they were new. You're also saying that the same $400,000 would have bought two, new $1000-tents every year since these were last used.

Well, all I've got to say is that you cynics are being entirely too cynical. A tent is something special, and I think, by George, we should all pitch in to help fix George's tents, so future generations of nose-picking, Bermuda-shorts-wearing, Interstate-highway-clogging tourists can gaze for a few minutes at a moldy piece of American History before waddling off to McDonald's for lunch.

THE BUCK NEVER GOT HERE

I plan to do my part by donating my tent to be used for display until George's are fixed. That is, if Dad can remember what he did with those wooden poles. And I also plan to go see the display in Yorktown, Virginia, as soon as I graduate from Antique Tent Repair School…

FISHING

FLY-FISHING—WITH A CAST OF THOUSANDS

John Jefferson once wrote, "To live life to its fullest, man must love...and fish." There's probably a lot of truth to that statement, just as there is to another one you've probably heard–"Give a man a fish and you feed him for a day. Teach a man to fish and you cause him to spend at least 15 percent of his annual adjusted gross income on fishing related products for the rest of his life."

These thoughts were running through my mind recently, as I read a letter I got from a fellow named Lefty Kreh. Maybe you've heard of Lefty. He is, after all, a world-famous fly-fishing expert who has fished with dukes and earls, kings and presidents, and is a victim of both the Great Depression and the Battle of the Bulge. That's what the letter said, anyway, and I don't doubt it for a minute.

There was a picture of Lefty in the letter. Ol' Lefty is built like a truck driver with a serious doughnut habit. Of course, a few extra pounds can be a tremendous advantage to a fly-fisherman. A little extra weight around the midsection gives a fellow a firm stance, enabling him to make a near perfect cast every time, which is very important, since about all a fly fisherman does is cast.

Anyway, the main point of Lefty's letter was that he wanted to teach me about fly-fishing. He's been teaching people about fly-fishing for many years, and he assured me in the letter that he could greatly improve my casting skills and cause me to catch a lot more fish.

Now, I appreciated Lefty's offer, but I doubt he could do me all that much good. He doesn't really have a lot to recommend him. How hard can it be to fish with kings, dukes, and presidents? All you have to do is make sure they catch more fish than you do so they'll look good, and I could probably handle that at my present level of expertise. Besides, I imagine the first thing Lefty would tell me to do would be gain forty or fifty pounds.

But the main reason I didn't bite Lefty's bait is because I already have a fly-fishing teacher. Leonard Wilson, the high school principal at Menard, is probably one of the best fly-fishermen in Texas. He's been fly-fishing since he was five years old, at which time he had to tie sandbags around his waist in order to get a firm enough stance to make a perfect cast. Leonard no longer has that problem. He now resembles Lee Trevino, only hairier.

Leonard had been telling me for years that he was going to take me fishing with him, and when I finally got a chance to go, I was overwhelmed with the amount of knowledge he tried to impart to me. The lesson started before we even left his house.

"Look here," Leonard said, pointing the remote control at the TV. "I can get *Wheel of Fortune* three times in a row, every evening, and they're all different."

We did, however, eventually make it to one of Leonard's private fishing holes, the location of which will remain a well-guarded secret until the day I die, or until someone offers me ten bucks, whichever comes first.

The first thing Leonard had me do was hold the end of his line so he could run about fifty feet of it off his reel and stretch it. Leonard treats his fly line the same way he treats the truth.

Then he led me over to an old johnboat that was lying overturned on the bank. It appeared to have been shot with a shotgun.

"What happened to the boat?" I asked.

"It got shot with a shotgun," Leonard said, "Here." He handed me a Clorox bottle and told me to cut the bottom out of it to bail the boat out with.

We finally put the boat in the water and paddled out a little way from shore, and Leonard told me to watch him for a while and he would show me how to cast. As it turns out, fly-fishing is pretty much what I thought it was.

What you do is you get out your tackle box and select a fly, which is like a lure, only smaller. Your fly needs to be very small so it won't attract any fish. Then you pull some line off your reel and start whipping your rod back and forth, like you're going to cast out in front of you, then behind you, then in front, etc. All the time you should be pulling more line off your reel, so the fly is going further and further in front and behind. You keep whipping the line back and forth for as long as you can.

The main thing to remember is whatever you do, *you must not let the fly touch the water.* This is called "dry-fly-fishing," and the fly must stay dry.

Besides, if the fly actually gets in the water, a fish might see it and try to eat it. It's a little known fact that fly-fishermen hate for a fish to get hung on their fly because then they have to reel in their line, get the fish off the hook, and start their cast all over again, thus wasting precious time that could be spent doing what they came to do—cast.

Leonard demonstrated his technique for several hours, and then told me I could quit paddling and use his extra fly rod and actually try my hand at casting a little bit. Of course, I didn't do nearly as well as Leonard. I let my fly fall into the water several times and even caught a couple of nice bass. Leonard was very nice about my mistakes, though, and acted like he didn't notice that I'd caught any fish. He was trying not to embarrass me.

THE BUCK NEVER GOT HERE

Anyway, thanks, Lefty, but no thanks. The next time I feel the need to go fly-fishing, I'll lie down and put a wet rag on my forehead until the urge passes...

THE YOUNG MAN AND THE TANK

No doubt you've heard the old saying that if you give a boy a fish, you feed him for a day; if you take three boys fishing, you're liable to wind up with a hook in your ear. This is what I was thinking a while back when my wife and I loaded up our three sons and went fishing at a tank with some friends.

It came to my attention recently that tank fishing is not as widely practiced as I thought it was. For those of you who are unfamiliar with tank fishing, I'll explain. Tank fishing is, contrary to the implication of the name, fishing in a tank, as opposed to a lake or river or bathtub. It incorporates all the advantages of lake or river fishing, such as mosquitoes, and mud, and poisonous snakes, without the unpleasantness, such as catching a lot of fish.

One of the main problems with our family fishing trips is the vast difference of opinions involved, concerning what items are absolutely essential, and what can be done without. I always want to take the bare essentials, since I'm the one who has to load everything up, unload it at the fishing hole, arrange it all according to instructions, load it back up, and unload it again at home. It's not unusual for me to argue, with firm conviction, that I can see no reason why everyone fishing needs to have their own rod and reel.

My wife, on the other hand, wants to take a seven-course meal, chairs for everyone, tables, tablecloths, napkins, disposable utensils, an umbrella, thirty pounds of ice, and a change of clothes for everyone. Somewhere in between there is a happy medium. This is never reached.

The boys don't want to load anything before the trip, they just want to go. They whine and complain the whole time their parents are arguing about what to take, wondering how they ever managed to get hooked up with such a disagreeable species. Of course, when they get to the water they want rods, reels, bait, and food to miraculously materialize. And a boat.

The subject of a boat never comes up until the pickup is completely loaded, and then it's always decided that, well, it really would be nice to have a boat, just in case. So I have to take everything out of the pickup, load the boat, and put everything back in. By this time, I'm generally pushing for a fishing trip to the bathtub.

The tank we were recently invited to fish is conveniently located in the middle of a large pasture at the end of a "road" containing boulders the size of a hall closet and gullies that will produce echoes. My wife spent the trip pointing out rocks and holes I would have had to be blind not to see. The fact that I had been fishing at this tank and driving this road for over twenty years made no difference to her.

As you know if you've ever fished a tank, bringing bait is totally unnecessary. Tanks, and their surroundings, contain an abundance of grasshoppers, small

THE BUCK NEVER GOT HERE

frogs, minnows, and other creatures that can be used for bait. The only problem with this is that my three boys are deeply into bugs, snakes, spiders, lizards, frogs, toads, and wollyworms. They very much enjoy catching these critters, but they don't want them harmed in any way. So when I tried to impale a small frog on a hook, Courtland, my eight-year-old, pitched a wall-eyed fit.

"DON'T PUT THAT FROG ON THAT HOOK!" he yelled, using capital letters for emphasis. He grabbed the frog away from me and held it protectively.

I tried to reason with him by explaining that, in nature, we're all part of the food chain, and that frogs, unfortunately, hold a pretty low position in this hierarchy. He set his jaw and held the frog further away from me, as if I might try to snatch it from him. His two brothers came and stood on either side of him, looking at me like I had suggested taking Hank the Cowdog to the pound. The frog, for his part, kept his mouth shut, but could have received an academy award for portraying an innocent victim.

Clearly, I had a problem. Never mind the inconsistency of protecting one creature while attempting to suffocate another by jerking it bodily out of its natural environment. Mr. Frog Travolta was not about to become dinner for a catfish, and I knew the same thing would happen if I tried to bait a hook with a grasshopper or minnow.

Luckily, I had brought a small box of fly-fishing flies along, and I tied one of these onto each of the

153

KENDAL HEMPHILL

boys' fishing lines. They were soon fishing happily, except for brief periods when they tried to beat each other to death with their rods. Three-year-old Leret even caught his first fish, a four-inch perch, which he proudly displayed to everyone present. He finally stuck it in the chest pocket of his bib overalls and wouldn't let anyone take it out. His mother had to wait until he fell asleep on the way home to remove it.

All in all, we had a wonderful time and everything went smoothly, despite the cooler getting knocked over and all our drinks and ice being spilled in the dirt, and the boys falling in the mud several times, and a couple of older boys who were there turning a canoe over in the tank and nearly drowning, and my wife getting melted marshmallow all in her hair. But the best part of the whole trip, the part that made it all worthwhile, was watching a little boy catch his first fish. That and not getting hooked in the ear...

ANIMALS

NEVER LET A WILD ANIMAL BACK YOU INTO A CORNER

If you've ever had your ferret family seized, then you should be able to sympathize with the guy in Delano, California, who wrote to Ann Landers recently and informed her that the California Department of Fish and Game came into his home and took away his ferrets. It's evidently illegal to keep ferrets as pets in California, since they are classified as wild animals.

This was, I'm sure, a crushing blow to Larry, the ferret owner, who says he loved Esther, Eleanor, and Bubba (yes, Bubba) almost like children. I can understand how he felt. I love my children almost like ferrets. The fact remains, however, that Larry should have checked to make sure it was legal to own ferrets in California *before* he got them.

I'm pretty sure ferrets can be legally owned in Texas because my friend, Harold Myers, used to have a European ferret named Judy. She was a fun pet, although all I can really remember that she ever did was poop in every corner of every room in the house. You could always tell when she was on a mission because she would run to a corner and turn around and back into it. This is not what I would call a desirable trait in a pet, but it made for some interesting entertainment. We'd be sitting in the living room, watching TV, when Harold would suddenly yell, "No, Judy!" and run and pick her up and try to get her to the litter box before she dropped her bomb. He was successful about half the time.

Anyway, in defense of Larry, I'd say ferrets are pretty tame "wild animals," compared to the pets some people own. A guy who used to live near Mason kept a mountain lion in his backyard.

I was unaware of this fact when I went to see this man. There was no answer to my knock at the door, so I walked around to the end of the house, and as I was about to round the corner into the backyard, I noticed the cougar lying on top of a rail fence at the rear of the yard. She was staring at me in a hungry manner, licking her lips and twitching her tail, but she was wearing a heavy collar with a chain attached, and I felt relieved to see that. Then I noticed that the chain was attached to a heavy wire that it could slide along, and I followed the

THE BUCK NEVER GOT HERE

wire from the tree at the back of the yard up to where it was attached to the house, two feet above my head.

You've probably seen cartoons, such as the *Flintstones*, in which a character levitates while his legs become a blurry ball before he shoots off at warp speed. You could've seen me do that in real life if you'd been with me that day. I made the three miles back to town in about two minutes. I went back later to get my pickup.

Of course, there's a reason why people shouldn't keep wild animals as pets. Not long ago, Mark McDonald wrote an article in the *San Antonio Express News* about deer attacking people, and one of the people attacked was Bobby Greenwade, who used to live in Mason County. His wife, Cynthia, could even be said to be responsible for this column, since she taught me to type in high school. Try not to hold it against her.

Mark's story included some harrowing tales of people being gored by crazed whitetail bucks, but strangely, he didn't mention poodles even once. I'm sure you find this as difficult to believe as I do, in light of the recent article in the *National Examiner* about a Milwaukee, Wisconsin resident named, seriously, John Hwilka, who was fatally shot in the chest with a .45 pistol by his poodle. The article said John was kneeling, showing his mother how to load the pistol, when the dog jumped on him and caused the gun to go off. Right. That's exactly what the poodle wants us to believe. Personally, I think the poodle's actions were intentional, and I think the motive was revenge.

Consider how you'd feel if you were forced to go out in public with one of those stupid, sissy-looking haircuts that poodle owners inflict on their pets. If I were a poodle, I would constantly be watching for a chance to get my paws on a firearm. We can only hope no one in charge of a nuclear missile silo ever decides to take his poodle to work with him, to keep him company. Sooner or later, the Brady Bill will be modified to include a provision prohibiting the sale of any firearm to a poodle owner.

In the interest of accurate reporting, though, I should mention that the article in the *Examiner* about the killer poodle also includes a story about a woman in Erie, Pennsylvania, whose pig saved her life. Lulu, a 150-pound Vietnamese potbellied pig, noticed her owner having a heart attack at her trailer house. The pig dialed 911 and performed CPR until paramedics arrived.

Just kidding! Actually, the story says the pig went out of the trailer house through a doggie door and laid down in the road in front of a car to get it to stop. Then she led the driver to the house to save her owner. Which just goes to prove what I've said all along—a pig is a much safer pet to have than a poodle. You almost never hear of a pig shooting its owner.

No doubt you've noted that there have been no incidents recently, pro or con, involving pet possums. This subject is of particular interest to me, since I personally happen to be a possum owner. My friend, Johnny Fleming, gave me a baby possum several months ago, having rescued it, along with about a dozen others, from the pouch of its mother, who was KIA while invading a trash can.

My family named our possum Pogo, and he happens to be the only one of the bunch to have survived. My wife fed him with an eyedropper until he got big enough to eat cat food, and he's been growing by leaps, and of course bounds, ever since. He's as gentle as a house cat, with thick, soft fur, no doubt due to the expensive cat food he eats.

Rest assured, however, that I am not fooled. I know the dangers of keeping a "wild animal" as a pet are always present. To avoid a possible tragedy, I make sure Pogo is never near any type of weapon... or a corner either...

LIVING THE WILD LIFE IN THE SUBURBS

Even if you're not really the outdoors type, you probably enjoy getting the chance to see wild animals occasionally, as long as they're not in your bedroom. Granted, you probably don't consider your bedroom to be wildlife habitat, unless it's really big and has lots of houseplants in it, but then, neither did my friend, Eric.

Eric is a single fellow who lives alone in an apartment complex near the San Angelo Country Club. He had just gotten out of the shower one evening when he heard a loud crash in his bedroom. He opened the door to see what was going on and there stood a whitetail doe. She had evidently come in through the window without bothering to open it, and poked her head through the screen, which was still hanging around her neck. She had cut herself on the window, and there was blood all over the place. Eric shut the bedroom door. Then he called 911.

When the police, firefighters, and EMS arrived, they found Eric standing in the living room, wearing a towel, babbling about a deer in his bedroom, where all his clothes were. After evicting the deer, the 911 folks decided it had been trying to get out of town, saw the reflection of the grass and bushes in the window of Eric's apartment, and jumped through the window.

This sort of thing doesn't happen every day, but it's probably more common than you might think. The August 1998 edition of *Reader's Digest* contains an article written by Anthony Brandy entitled "When Nature Comes Too Close," which says wildlife is moving into the suburbs all over the U.S., and causing a lot of damage. Hunting restrictions and game management programs have caused the populations of certain animals to rise dramatically, and they're having to move into town with us.

For instance, in a western Massachusetts town, a black bear recently came through a screen door, grabbed a bag of candy bars off the kitchen table, and fled. While I'm sure the owners of the house probably frowned on this type of animal behavior, especially if they were eating supper at the time, I think we can all agree that having a bear steal your candy bars is, by far, preferable to what happened to my friend Elvis Martin several years ago right here in Mason, Texas.

THE BUCK NEVER GOT HERE

Elvis lived with his wife, his stepson, and a large rat. Most people who saw this rat thought, at first, that it was a small dog. Elvis kept a pellet gun in the living room, in hopes of getting a decent shot at it. This was a really big rat. A rat's rat.

Joel Draper was at Elvis' house one evening watching TV when the rat jumped on top of the refrigerator, grabbed a loaf of bread, and pulled it to the floor with him. He then started down the hall, with the bread, toward his escape hole, with Elvis in hot pursuit, pumping up the pellet gun. He never got a shot, but the bread was rescued because it wouldn't go through the hole. The perpetrator had to abandon it to get away.

What strikes me as odd is that while no one would object to killing a rat that has developed the habit of stealing the Butter Krust off someone's refrigerator, a lot of people think it's wrong to shoot deer who are destroying private property and causing a great deal of costly damage.

Anthony's article in *Reader's Digest* states that the folks in North Haven, New York, which occupies a 2.5-square-mile peninsula off Long Island, are having a lot of trouble with deer eating their ornamental shrubbery, etc. They've been trying to figure out a way to control these deer for a long time, and one of the solutions they came up with was (you'd better sit down before you read this) contraception.

No doubt you think I'm making this up, unless you've read the article yourself. I read it three times, and I'm still having trouble keeping a straight face.

The deer, evidently, could not be expected to submit to the contraceptives voluntarily, so the plan was to vaccinate them with a dart gun. Each deer would have had to be vaccinated twice a year, at $200 a pop, and the deer would have had to be tagged to keep hunters from eating the vaccine. Otherwise, I suppose, any woman who ate venison from North Haven would never again be able to give birth to a fawn.

The problem, as I see it, is not that there are too many deer in urban areas, but that there is a branch of the Humane Society called the "Urban Wildlife Protection Program." The director of this program, John Hadidian, says they need "a whole new science to understand what the problems are in the suburbs—and to figure out what to do."

I know what you're thinking. You're thinking, "Why don't they just issue a certain number of 'archery only' deer permits each year? This would solve the deer population problem, create some revenue for the state, and allow some hunters to put some high-quality, low-fat meat in their freezers."

While this would seem, on the surface, to be the perfect solution to the problem, when studied extensively, it becomes clear that this would be the perfect solution to the problem.

But it's too easy. The Urban Wildlife Protection People would never go for it because it gives them no chance to appear to care deeply about these animals. Besides, without an urban deer problem, there would be no need for an Urban Wildlife Protection Program.

THE BUCK NEVER GOT HERE

So, if you live in an urban area, try not to run over any deer on your way to work. It throws the stats out of kilter. And if you're in a drugstore and a ten-point buck walks in making threatening gestures with his antlers, give him the contraceptives ...

THE STRAIGHT POOP ON BATS

The Festival of St. Vincent is a national holiday held each year in the country of Luxemburg, which, I believe, is somewhere near Europe. The participants begin the festivities by dropping a live goat from the top of a church tower into a blanket.

The World Championship Barbeque Goat Cook-Off is an annual competition held every Labor Day weekend in Brady, Texas, which is in the United States. The participants begin the festivities by dropping a live Frenchman from the top of the McCulloch County courthouse into a handkerchief.

Not really. The participants actually just show up at Richard's Park and start cooking. It would be much more interesting if they dropped a goat into a barbecue pit or something, but they don't. I intend to check with the Goat Cook-Off officials and see if something can be done about this.

Of course, the animal rights people would probably have something to say about a goat being dropped, whether it was actually damaged or not. Folks are sensitive about that sort of thing in America. You can say what you want about the people in Luxemburg, but at least they don't let anyone tell them what they can do with their goats.

In the USA, however, we have to be a little more careful what we do and say when it comes to animals. Kick a dog around, and you're liable to find yourself in Big Trouble. And this attitude is not restricted to just pet-type animals. Even creatures that most people would rather not have around most of the time have supporters.

Take bats, for instance. Your average American would probably just as soon not have anything to do with bats but, according to some folks, we couldn't get along without them.

My friend, Matt Anderson, otherwise known as Batman, was the steward at the Eckert James River Bat Cave for two years. The Bat Cave is located about twenty miles southeast of Mason, Texas, and belongs to the Texas Nature Conservancy. Visitors can go and watch the bats emerge from the cave Thursday through Sunday evenings starting at about six o'clock.

Bats are very interesting creatures, and they eat lots of mosquitoes and other bugs, and the world would basically fold up on us if they were to disappear, according to Matt. The bats at the James River Bat Cave are Mexican Free-Tailed bats, and they migrate back and forth between Texas and Mexico, which means that toward the end of October, they will fly south again. Sort of like Yankees heading for Florida every year.

Another interesting bat fact is that there are some valuable uses for bat poop. The six million bats at the

THE BUCK NEVER GOT HERE

James River Bat Cave deposit a staggering amount of guano in the cave every summer, and Matt sometimes dug some of it out, bagged it up, and gave it to people for use on their lawns and gardens because it is supposedly an outstanding fertilizer.

In fact, so many people asked Matt for bat guano he decided that since he was going to be driving his pickup in the annual Jaycee Round-Up Parade in Mason last July, ostensibly as a float, he would accommodate folks and throw baggies of bat guano out as he went around the square. So, while the people on the other (real) floats threw candy and gum, Matt flung little plastic bags full of bat poop at the cheering crowds.

The parade always makes two laps around the town square. Everything went well on the first round, and Matt was just about out of poop bags when the parade started its second trip around town. It soon became apparent that the folks weren't quite as excited about being bombarded with bat poop as Matt thought they would be. They started throwing it back, and he had to roll up his windows to keep out the little brown bags that came flying at him from all directions. I guess some people just can't appreciate good poop.

But fertilizer and projectile material are not the only uses for bat poop. One of the main ingredients in mascara is bat guano. That's right, you ladies are walking around town, going to work, attending parties, and actually eating meals with bat poop on your eyelashes.

Disgusting, isn't it? And I'm not even going to mention what lipstick is made from …

GUNS

GUN CLEANING MADE DIFFICULT

We live in a disposable society. Not that society itself can be thrown away, although that might seem like a good idea sometimes, but an awful lot of the things we use every day are made to be used once or twice and discarded. "One-time-use" diapers, plates, cups, napkins, and similar items have been available for a long time, but lately many more, larger utensils have become disposable.

Not so long ago, if your television quit working, you took it to a repair shop and got it fixed. Now, if your TV quits, you'll do well to get someone with a pulse on the phone when you call the customer service department of the company who made it, and you can forget finding anyone who will actually fix your set. It's easier to just chunk it and go buy another one. vcrs, microwaves, hair dryers, electric razors, and many other items are the same way.

Guns, however, are not, and will probably never be, offered in a disposable version. And since guns get dirty with use, they have to be cleaned once in a while. The normal shooter must periodically clean his guns to remove dirt and dust that have accumulated in all the cracks and crevices, and also to remove the unburned powder that can gunk up a rifle or pistol with use.

Of course, children should never have free access to firearms, not only because of the safety factor, but also because of what they might do to the guns. If you, like many Americans, have small children in your household, watch them for a while and see how they treat toys and appliances, and you'll see what I mean. My kids regularly try to insert peanut butter and jelly sandwiches into the vcr. My boots, which usually sit in my closet minding their own business, are a prime target. Before I put them on, I turn them upside down and make sure there are no Cheerios, marbles, or artificial bait in them. There's no telling what my boys would do to my guns if they got hold of them.

Anyway, in the interest of humanitarism, I've decided to offer some helpful hints about cleaning firearms. Some people, I've noticed, avoid this type of job if at all possible. That's to be expected, since gun cleaning can be a messy, meticulous chore, but it doesn't have to

THE BUCK NEVER GOT HERE

be. Just follow these helpful hints, and your next gun cleaning session will be a breeze.

First, you must determine how often a gun should be cleaned. This is, for the most part, a judgment call. Some people clean their guns after every use, but your firearms experts, such as myself, frown on this type of behavior. If you clean your gun too often, you'll end up rubbing the bluing off and have to take it to your local gunsmith to have it reblued. Then there are those who never clean their guns and then wonder why they finally quit working altogether. Somewhere in the middle, there is a happy medium. I recommend cleaning the average firearm once every five years, or right before you take it to a gun show to trade it off, whichever comes first.

When you determine that a gun needs cleaning, the most important factor to consider is whether or not your wife is at home. This may seem like a minor detail, but it's often the little things that make all the difference. It's best to wait until your spouse will be out of town for several days if you intend to clean more than two or three guns at once. Women tend to get upset over the tiniest discrepancies, such as Hoppe's #9 in the carpet, or grease in the silverware drawer. And wives can be very distracting, prohibiting the type of concentration required for adequate firearm maintenance.

After your wife leaves the house, clear off the kitchen table. Those of you who have workshops or gunrooms may want to clean your guns somewhere else, but I've never found any place as suitable for gun cleaning as the kitchen table. Sort of gives the job a homey feel.

Lay your gun on the table and stare at it for a while, taking care to note any distinguishing marks or scratches that may not have been there the last time the gun was cleaned. Also, inspect the gun carefully to ensure that it belongs to you. This is very important, because if you suddenly remember borrowing the gun from a friend, you'll want to immediately return it and let the friend do the cleaning.

Another important consideration is making sure the gun is unloaded before you start. I can't overstress how tragic it would be to have your gun accidentally discharge and shoot a valuable bullet into the dishwasher, especially if it was a carefully hand-loaded cartridge. There's just no sense in wasting good ammunition, so make sure the breech is clear to begin with.

Knowing the requirements of the particular weapon to be cleaned is also essential. My first rifle was a Remington Nylon 66 .22, which my dad bought for me in San Antonio when I was about twelve. I had watched my friends take their Nylon 66s apart many times, and on the way home to Mason, I decided to disassemble my new rifle in the backseat of the car. What I didn't know was that you have to cock a Nylon 66 before you take it apart, or else 487 pounds of force is required to get the thing back together. For an hour and a half, I fought to put my brand-new, never-fired gun back together, knowing that at any time my parents would turn around and find out I had ruined it before I even

THE BUCK NEVER GOT HERE

got it home. When we were ten miles from Mason, my adrenaline had built up to the point where, with superhuman strength, I finally mashed all the parts back in. I was never so scared in my life. Well, I seem to have run out of time here, which is what usually happens when I start to clean a gun. I'll have to finish my gun cleaning tips next week. I hate to put something off, but this is what usually happens when I start to clean a gun…

GUN CLEANING MADE MONOTONOUS
THE SAGA CONTINUES

Last week, we took the first step in the important process of gun cleaning, namely deciding whether to actually clean a gun. The first step in any endeavor is usually the most important and often the most difficult. Like the old Chinese proverb says, "The longest journey begins with a single step." Which is pretty silly when you think about it, since cleaning a gun has nothing to do with taking a long journey, or even a short one. Forget I mentioned it.

The important thing to remember in gun cleaning is that keeping your gun clean and properly maintained will ensure that it will function as intended for a lifetime, or until the space cadets you've elected to congress decide you can't be trusted with firearms and take them all away, whichever comes first. So you should always keep your guns in good working order, in case you need to use them to protect your constitutional right to keep and bear them.

We covered the prerequisites necessary to cleaning a gun last week, such as making sure your wife is not at home, and your gun is unloaded, so let's get right to the nitty gritty, so to speak, of gun cleaning.

Your gun, like every other gun, is a particular caliber. Unless it is a gauge. It has to be either a caliber or a gauge because those are the only two ways gun manufacturers determine how much to charge when selling a gun. Before you can clean your gun, you need to figure out what caliber or gauge it is.

To determine the caliber or gauge of your gun, stick your fingers, one at a time, into the hole in the end of the barrel. Stop when you get to the finger that will barely go in the hole. If the finger is your thumb, then it is not a finger, and your gun is probably a 12 gauge. This gun has such a large hole that the gun rarely needs cleaning, and I recommend putting it back in the gun cabinet.

Once you figure out which finger fits in the barrel of your gun, you need to go to your local gun store and buy a gun-cleaning kit. The kit should contain a steel, tubular-shaped brush about the same size as the finger that fits in the barrel. Or you can use the wimp method and look on the side of the gun and read the numbers stamped there, and buy a kit with the same numbers written on the box.

Your gun-cleaning kit should also have some rods in it, and the rods should be about a foot long. One of them should have a handle on one end, and all the rods should screw together. There should also be some other attachments in the kit. These are unnecessary. The mak-

THE BUCK NEVER GOT HERE

ers of gun-cleaning kits only put them in there so they can charge you more for the kit.

Take your cleaning kit home and open it up on the kitchen table. Screw the brush onto one of the rods and attach the rest of the rods together. You should end up with one long rod with a brush on one end and a handle on the other.

Start poking the brush down the barrel of the gun and pulling it back out. Do this until you get tired of it, and then wrap a small piece of cloth, called a cleaning patch (which should have come in your kit) around the brush. Apply a light coat of Hoppe's Powder Solvent #9 to the patch, spilling a liberal amount of solvent on the table. Run the brush in and out of the barrel a few times, and then get a new patch and repeat. You should do this, according to the instructions in the kit, until you can run a clean patch through the barrel and not get it dirty. This is merely a sadistic joke being played on you by the people who made the kit. Your patch will never come out clean. Just run each patch in and out of the barrel about ten times, and quit when you've used 12,347 patches.

This should take care of just about any modern-type firearm, but if the gun you wish to clean is a muzzleloader, you'll need to go about it in a totally different way. Contrary to what you may have heard, muzzleloaders are not really firearms at all. They are part of a nefarious plan developed by anti-hunters to thin the ranks of their opposition. It's going pretty well.

The easiest way to keep a muzzleloader clean is not to shoot it at all. If you insist on firing one of these weapons, by the time you finish cleaning it, you will regret your decision.

The first step in cleaning a muzzleloader is to remove the barrel from the stock. This is easy to do, since a muzzleloader is basically waiting for a chance to fall apart. All you have to do is extract the keeper bar from the forearm of the stock, and the barrel will easily fall onto your toe. It weighs thirty-seven pounds.

Take the barrel and limp into the bathroom. Fill the bathtub about six inches deep with hot water, pour in some Epsom salts, and soak your toe for thirty minutes. Drain the tub, refill to the same level with very hot water, and pour in some soap. Stand the barrel upright in the tub, pointing up. Fill the barrel with water from the tub, and lay a patch on top. Screw a "jag" onto your cleaning rod and use it to push the patch all the way down into the barrel, and run it in and out for a while. Change patches every ten strokes, and change the water in the barrel every thirty strokes. Do this until you have made some impressive scratches in the enamel of the bathtub, which shouldn't take too long, judging from my own experience. When your shoulders turn blue, give it up. No one, to my knowledge, has ever gotten a muzzleloader clean. Pour the water out of the barrel, run a few dry patches through, then an oily one, and quit.

So there you have it. By following my step-by-step procedure, you should have no trouble at all cleaning your favorite firearm. Just remember: That first step is usually the one that gets you into trouble...

THE BUCK NEVER GOT HERE

THE AVALANCHE HAS STARTED–IT IS
TOO LATE FOR THE PEBBLES TO VOTE

I can't remember where I heard the title of this column, but it seems to fit our current situation fairly well. The recent tragedy at Columbine High School in Littleton, Colorado, is the latest event in a downward spiral the United States has been in for a long time.

The easy response after such a devastating, horrible occurrence is to look for someone to blame, other than, of course, those who actually perpetrated the crime. Although the two teenagers are obviously guilty themselves, there is no dearth of psychologists, psychiatrists, and psychoanalysts who can come up with numerous other culprits skulking around behind the scenes to point their overeducated fingers at. According to a good portion of the media, depending on which newspaper or magazine you happen to read today, there are more guilty parties than you can shake a stick at.

Some say the boys' parents are to blame for not keeping a tighter rein on their offspring. Some blame the violent movies and television shows kids currently watch. Some say this event was brought about by the kind of music teenagers are listening to today. Others are exhuming Friedrich Nietzsche, the nineteenth-century German philosopher whose nihilism was fleshed out by the Nazis fifty years ago. Some blame society in general.

By far, the lion's share of the accusations has been aimed at guns. This is to be expected. Every crime in which a firearm is used gives the anti-gun people more ammunition. It doesn't seem to matter that the guns used in the Littleton tragedy, sawed-off shotguns and "machine guns" (fully automatic weapons), have been illegal (without a permit) in this country since 1934. I shouldn't have to mention that pipe bombs are also illegal. Federal law also prohibits anyone under the age of eighteen from owning or possessing a handgun, and doesn't allow anyone of any age to carry a firearm within 1,000 feet of a school.

In light of these facts, it's evident that the boys who walked into Columbine High School and started shooting their classmates violated an awful lot of laws. This proves a law is only effective when citizens choose to obey it.

Criminals, by definition, are people who don't choose to obey the laws. We already have enough gun laws to choke the democrat donkey, but there will always be those who ignore them. Cesare Beccaria, the famed eighteenth-century Italian criminologist, once said, "Laws that forbid the carrying of arms... disarm only those who are neither inclined nor determined to commit crimes."

Beccaria's views seem to have been borne out by the crime rate in Australia over the past year. About a year ago, Australia, having no Second Amendment, banned nearly all types of firearms. The country had enjoyed a steady decrease in gun-related crimes over the previous twenty-five years, and those in authority hoped to further enhance the safety of its citizens by spending $500 million and destroying over 640,000 firearms.

THE BUCK NEVER GOT HERE

It didn't work. During the past year, armed robberies have increased 44 percent , homicides went up 3.2 percent, and there were 8.6 percent more assaults than the year before. There has been a dramatic increase in break-ins and assaults on the elderly, and the state of Victoria alone has seen 300 percent more homicides involving guns.

What went wrong? Australian politicians haven't been able to figure it out, and their only response to this question has been that they need to "give it more time." At least it's encouraging to know that not all the idiot politicians are in Washington, D.C.

The framers of the Constitution of the United States didn't include the Second Amendment in the Bill of Rights by accident. Patrick Henry said, "The great object is that every man be armed... Everyone who is able may have a gun."

It's obvious, however, that our forefathers weren't trying to protect our right to keep and bear arms just so we could protect ourselves from the criminal element. They evidently had bigger game in mind—our government itself.

James Madison, fourth president of the U.S., said, "Americans have the advantage of being armed—which they possess over the people of Europe, where the governments are afraid to trust the people with arms." Why else but to ensure against revolution would a government be afraid of having armed citizens?

George Madison, the father of the Bill of Rights, said, "To disarm the people is the best and most effective way to enslave them."

Thomas Jefferson said, "The strongest reason for the people to retain the right to keep and bear arms is, as a last resort, to protect themselves against tyranny in government."

Joseph Story, a u.s. Supreme Court Justice, said, "One of the ordinary modes, by which tyrants accomplish their purpose without resistance, is by disarming the people, and making it an offense to keep arms…"

I could go on quoting famous, respected people, but none of this carries much weight with the anti-gunners. They want to, eventually, make it illegal to own any type of firearm, and the senseless episode in Littleton is one more bullet in their gun, so to speak.

What bothers me is not that there are those who want to take guns away from the people, but that we've allowed them to get such a good start. Hunters don't need fully automatic weapons, so when our government decided to ban them from private ownership we said, "That's OK. We don't need those anyway. Let them have those, and they'll leave us alone."

The problem is not only that once the camel's nose is under the tent, the rest of him is sure to follow, but that "assault"-type weapons are the ones most protected by the Second Amendment. They're the ones we would need the most should we be forced to, as Thomas Jefferson put it, "protect ourselves against tyranny in government."

I guess, considered in that light, it was logical that the government took those guns first. Now, which one of us pebbles even has a ballot?

"First they came for the Jews"

In Germany they first came for the Communists

And I didn't speak up because I wasn't a Communist.

Then they came for the Jews,

And I didn't speak up because I wasn't a Jew.

Then they came for the trade unionists

And I didn't speak up because I wasn't a trade unionist.

Then they came for the Catholics

And I didn't speak up because I was a Protestant.

Then they came for me

And by that time no one was left to speak up.

—Pastor Neirnoller

BILL OF RIGHTS OR BILL OF WRONGS?

It seems common sense is pretty uncommon these days. We live in the greatest country in the world (America), yet even here, it's necessary to put a warning label on a toaster that says: "To avoid serious injury, do not poke a butter knife down in one of these slots while operating."

Take, for instance, our Constitution. I realize our founding fathers understood the Constitution would have to be updated. They knew they weren't perfect, and that situations would arise in the future that they hadn't thought of, so they made provision for amendments to be attached to the main law that governs our society.

The first ten of these amendments are known as the Bill of Rights. Obviously, pretty quick after the ink dried saying that all men were created equal, someone decided he was a little more equal than the average bear. So the bill of rights was written, in clear, concise language, to safeguard our freedom of religion, freedom of speech, right to keep and bear arms, etc. This is why it is perfectly legal for us to carry our guns around with us everywhere we ...

Oops! I forgot; our right to keep and bear arms, which our forefathers promised to preserve for us in the Constitution, was infringed, and a long time ago, too. I guess someone lost sight of the fact that if private citizens had never been allowed to own and use guns, we would be British.

Of course, if you would like to exercise your right to carry a gun around with you, which has already been guaranteed to you, the state of Texas has provided a way for you to do that.

First, you have to take a class to learn about a great many laws which you have been breaking already, since you're not silly enough to travel around without a weapon. This class will cost you about $100. Then, you have to send off for a "packet" that has a lot of papers in it that have to be filled out properly and mailed to the State Official In Charge of Properly Filled-Out Papers. You also have to send this person a check for $140. If every t is crossed and you're lucky, you will receive a

THE BUCK NEVER GOT HERE

five-year license that says you can carry a concealed handgun around with you, even to the bathroom. Thus, if you wish, you can spend your own, hard-earned, u.s. dollars, and buy a right you already have.

This worries me. I understand the people in charge think they are protecting us when they pass laws that say we can't carry our guns around, even though we have the right to. They think that, if we don't have guns, we won't shoot anybody. And they're right. No one had a gun in the McDonald's ("You Deserve a Break Today") restaurant when the disgruntled postal worker walked in and started shooting people with a shotgun. So no one shot him. And no one had a gun in the Luby's cafeteria where another man did the same thing, with several guns. Thank goodness the people in charge made those laws saying that honest, law-abiding citizens couldn't carry guns, or else one of those guys might have gotten hurt before he was able to kill a bunch of people. Obviously, in trying to protect us, our lawmakers have actually left us, as the saying goes, "between two fires." We either break the law or remain defenseless.

Of course, I'm glad that now, if some yahoo walks into a public eating joint and starts shooting, then someone else, who has a Concealed Handgun License, is liable to pull out a pistol and double tap said yahoo, hopefully before the yahoo shoots me or mine. I think this is a good law, and I hope every law-abiding citizen in Texas applies for and receives a license, and then carries a gun around with him or her. Because you can bet your last ruble the bad guys are already carrying guns around with them, license or no license.

What worries me about the Concealed Handgun License law is that, now that our protectors have figured out a way to make us pay for our right to keep and bear arms, they may decide to make us pay for our right to keep and bear legs too. For instance, they may decide to charge us by the letter for free speech. This would give new meaning to the phrase, "Pat, I'd like to buy a vowel."

About ten or twelve years ago, when the law was passed that said adults had to wear seat belts, Jack Cowan began his column in the *San Angelo Standard Times* with, "I *know* I should buckle my seat belt every time I get in my car. I *know* it can save my life. But I have a problem with my government telling me I have to do something for my own good, and that if I don't I'm violating the law." Jack went on to explain why whether we wear a seat belt is our own business, and not the government's. He ended the column with something like this: "I'm afraid that, if we let the seat belt law go through without complaint, in a few years I'll be starting a column with, 'I *know* I should brush my teeth after every meal… '"

Well, that's probably next. What it all boils down to is government control. The "of the people" is still in our Constitution, but the "by the people" is now "by the best liars," and the "for the people" is a joke.

Now, having complained about being forced to buy our right to keep and bear arms, I strongly urge all of

THE BUCK NEVER GOT HERE

you to do just that. Unless we take advantage of this opportunity, we will be unarmed, literally, to defend ourselves against further injustices. And if we don't take a stand now, in a year or two, Ol' Jack may be starting a column with, "I *know* I should wear clean underwear every time I go out…"

GENERAL

THE LONGEST DISTANCE BETWEEN TWO POINTS

One of the most valuable talents an outdoorsperson can have is the ability to keep from getting lost. If you've ever traveled off the trampled path, you know it's a terrible feeling to suddenly realize you have no idea which direction to go to get to the nearest Burger King.

Luckily, there are some precautions that can be taken to avoid losing your way in the wilderness. Since I happen to be an authority on the outdoors, people often ask me how they can keep from losing themselves. I've decided to give you readers the benefit of my

KENDAL HEMPHILL

expertise for free, but if you decide I'm being too generous, you're welcome to send me a large wad of money.

The easiest way to keep from getting lost in the woods is to stay out of the woods. This would seem to be obvious to any sane, rational person with an IQ higher than dried sausage, but you'd be surprised how many people go into forests with no regard for the fact that they will shortly want to come back out. There's a technical term used by search and rescue personnel for people who go into wilderness areas with no navigational skills whatever: *compost*.

If you're determined to travel into country where there are no roads or trails, you'll need to learn a few basic tricks so you can find your way home again. One is to always take someone along who can operate a compass.

You may think that, since there are no buttons, knobs, switches, or levers on a compass, one can be used by an average knothead such as yourself. This is not the case. I consider myself an average knothead, and I've never even figured out how to turn a compass on.

The magnetic compass was invented a long time ago in some specific year by the man whose name it bears: Walter P. Magnetic. Ever since then, people have been going into the wilderness in total confidence and, with the aid of their trusty compasses, getting lost and starving to death.

In order to understand how a compass is supposed to work, you should be aware that there are four major directions: left, right, up, and, of course, down. On a compass, these directions are denoted by four letters: W, E, N, and

THE BUCK NEVER GOT HERE

S. Those of you who are really sharp have already figured out that these letters stand for what are called the four points of the compass, namely left, right, up, and down. The letters also stand for west, east, north, and south, which are the four basic directions you may choose from to get from where you are to somewhere else.

This may sound relatively simple, and it would be, if these four directions were all there were. Unfortunately, there are a lot more directions, and none of them are indicated on your compass. There is south by southeast, west by southwest, east by northsouth, north by southeastwest, and *North by Northwest,* which is allowed to be capitalized, since it was made into a major motion picture starring Cary Grant. There are others, but I won't try to list them all, since I already have a headache.

A common misconception about compasses is that they will tell you which way to go. They won't. Many people who expected too much from their compasses have ended up hopelessly lost, and never found their way to the checkout counter at the sporting goods store to pay for their compasses. This is because, since there is a needle in the middle of a compass, people expect to be able to look at the needle and walk in the direction it is pointing to get where they want to go. This is fine if you want to go north, because your basic compass needle is supposed to point basically north. But if you want to go, say, east, you have to turn your compass until the needle points to the E, and go that way.

Another problem with compasses is that if you hold one too close to a magnet or a large piece of metal, or a newspaper columnist's head, the needle won't point in the right direction anymore. If your compass is really cheap, the needle may even bend into the shape of Roseanne Barr and spin around in circles.

So compasses are quite confusing by themselves, but they become even more so when you try to use one in conjunction with a map. Before you go into the woods, you need to obtain a map of the area you plan to get lost in. The hard part about using a map is figuring out where you are on it. To do this, you need to spread your map out on the ground with the left side of the map to your left, etc. Then you get down on your knees with your compass in your hand and look down at it, then at your map, then at your compass, and so on until your knees start to hurt. Then you fold up your map and take off in some random direction. Be very careful not to lose your map. Maps are extremely handy, especially if you plan to get lost during the winter, since you can use one to start a fire.

So you can see that using a compass for navigation is a pretty chancy business. After studying the matter thoroughly for the last twenty minutes, I think the best advice I can give you is this: throw your compass away. When you need guidance in the woods, spit in your left hand, make a fist with your right hand, and slam it down into your left. Go in whatever direction the spit goes. This is the method Lewis and Clark used on their famous expedition, and they made it home in just under two and a half years ...

THE MOST DUMBEST INVENTION OF
ALL TIME® BY KENDAL HEMPHILL®

A few minutes ago, I made an important discovery. I found out that my computer will make this symbol: ®. This is the trademark symbol required when you write the name of an item that is registered with the United States Bureau of Registered Things, such as Preparation H®, or Windows 95®, or Nolan Ryan®. This lets the typical bonehead consumer, such as yourself, know the item in question is registered, which is very important, at least to the company that makes the item.

As a professional journalist, I'm required to know this kind of thing, and use the ® symbol whenever it's required, so I don't irritate important people and get myself into hot water.

For instance, if I were to write, "Billy Bob was giving me a hard time, so I hit him over the head with my crescent wrench," I would be in violation of federal trademark laws, and unhappy men in ill-fitting suits might come and carry me off to jail and take away my birthday. The correct way to write that sentence would be, "Billy Bob was giving me a hard time, so I hit him over the head with my Crescent® wrench." That way, the worst that could happen is that Billy Bob might come to and beat the sap out of me with his Chevrolet® tire tool.

So, what the ® symbol basically does is keep the typical bonehead consumer from forgetting that Crescent® is a brand name, and not a type of wrench.

Granted, the typical bonehead consumer doesn't care beans about that, but the Crescent® company does, and it can sue me. I checked.

Of course, when the average consumer has his head under the average kitchen sink and asks his average wife to hand him a wrench, he doesn't say, "Honey, would you please hand me the Crescent® brand adjustable wrench by your left hand?" No, what he usually says is, "Gimme the crescent by your left hand. No, no, your *other* left hand!"

My point here is that although Crescent® is a brand name, the word *crescent* has become a generic term meaning 'adjustable wrench' because that's the way it has been used by the average consumer. And Crescent® isn't the only brand name that has been diluted this way. The same thing has happened to a lot of other terms that we use every day, and it's all my fault.

In a recent column I wrote I mentioned that Velcro was probably the greatest invention in the history of mankind. This was a major faux pas (pronounced *faux pas*). As a result of that article, I got a letter from Pamela J. Carter, a legal assistant who works for the VELCRO® people in Manchester, New Hampshire, explaining that my column "unfortunately misuses the registered trademark VELCRO®." I would have been better off, evidently, if I had written, "The most dumbest invention anybody ever came up with is VELCRO®." Then the VELCRO® people would have been happy, and I wouldn't have gotten into Hot Water®.

Actually, Pamela's letter was very nice, and pointed out that oversights such as mine weaken the identity and value

THE BUCK NEVER GOT HERE

of the "VELCRO® hook and loop fastener trademark." She also mentioned that *escalator, thermos, cellophane,* and *nylon* were all terms that were once trademarks, but have become generic because their owners allowed them to be misused by the public.

I realize no one wants to be the bearer of bad news, but someone needs to call Pam and let her know that she's a little late. I conducted a survey of a broad cross-section of the people who came into my office last Saturday, and I found that only about 3 percent of the American public knows that VELCRO® is a brand name. The term has already become generic. The only people who are still apparently unaware of this fact are the VELCRO® people.

But misusing the word *Velcro* wasn't the only mistake I made in that column. Pam also pointed out that VELCRO® was *not* invented for the Apollo® space program, as I said it was, although she acknowledged that many parts of space shuttle Columbia® are attached with their hook and loop fastener. She intimated that, if it weren't for VELCRO®, the shuttle's tail would probably fall off. At least that's the impression I got. Then she enlightened me as to the actual origin of VELCRO®.

It was invented, she said, by a bright fellow in Switzerland® named George de Mestral®, during the 1940s. George had a dog, probably one of those big, hairy ones with the little barrel of whiskey attached to his collar, and he liked to take this dog for walks in the woods.

One day, George noticed that cockleburs stuck to his clothing (as I said, George was bright), and he got to looking at the burrs under his microscope and drinking the whiskey straight out of the little barrel, and when he noticed how the little hooks on the burrs hung onto the little loops on his clothes, George passed out. Then he had a brilliant idea. He drew some diagrams and rushed right down to the nearest government patent office and registered his invention.

Unfortunately, Switzerland® had no space program, and no one was interested in a rocket made entirely of cockleburs. So it was another twenty years before George's invention was put to use.

Anyway, I appreciated Pam's letter, and from now on I intend to be very careful not to misuse a brand name. Just to be on the safe side, I plan to use the ® symbol any time I am in doubt, such as when I write things like Suppository® or Inflate-A-Potty®. You never know when you may be unintentionally contributing to the delinquency of a brand name.

And I wish someone who knows Pam® would give her a call and let her know she's trying to shut the barn door after the horse is gone on this VELCRO® business. While you're at it, you might mention that I write a Humor Column® and have no regard for Accuracy®, unless I can make fun of it...

BREATHING OXYGEN LINKED TO STAYING ALIVE

The other day, I walked into my bedroom and glanced over into the corner, where my desk is supposed to be, and it wasn't there. My wife had evidently been rearranging the furniture again. She does that periodically, although I've told her over and over that if God had

THE BUCK NEVER GOT HERE

wanted her to move furniture, he would have given her a hairy chest and pants that wouldn't stay up in back. I always end up walking into walls and skinning my shins when I get up in the middle of the night after one of her sprees.

"Honey," I called, "where did you move my desk to?"

"It's right there where it's always been," she said, "under that big pile of papers. Your desk looks like the professor's in the *Shoe* cartoon."

I looked, and sure enough, there was a huge pile of papers in the corner of the room. I dug a while and found my desk, my computer, and Jimmy Hoffa.

Not really! Jimmy Hoffa was under the bed. But I did clean my desk off and find my computer and some other stuff, including some interesting junk mail.

One of the letters I found is from a company called Oxygenation Systems of Texas, which is based in Anahuac (civic motto: Y'all Come Back to Anahuac).

The letter is an ad for something called the Oxygen Edge, which is a device invented by a fellow named David Kinser, who obviously has a great deal of spare time. The Oxygen Edge is supposed to help fishermen keep fish alive in live wells, which is evidently a problem, especially during the hot summer months.

If you're not a fisherman, this probably requires an explanation. See, when a bass fisherman is fishing, he puts the fish he catches in a live well, which is sort of like a bucket of water in a boat, except it costs a lot more money. Bass fishermen don't like anything that doesn't cost a lot of money.

An angler can only kill a certain number of fish per day, and this number is called a limit. When the fisherman gets a limit of fish in his live well, he throws the smallest one back into the lake, so he can legally keep fishing. This is called boredom, and it is brought on by overexposure to sunlight and fishing shows on TV.

The problem is that when the weather gets extremely hot, the fish in the live well tend to go belly up due to a shortage of oxygen in the water, which causes the fisherman to have to quit fishing. This would seem to most people a blessing, but bass fishermen hate to have to quit fishing. I guess they believe that sooner or later, if they keep at it long enough, they'll start to have fun. This is called dreaming.

Another important reason to keep fish alive in live wells is that, in order to be a valid entry in a bass fishing tournament, a fish cannot be dead. And since thousands of dollars are at stake in many tournaments, fishermen are very interested in keeping their fish alive. It is not uncommon at such an event to see a grown man crying while holding a dead fish that, if still alive, would have won him a bass boat the size of space shuttle Columbia. Mouth-to-gill resuscitation has been tried, unsuccessfully, more than once.

So I wasn't really surprised to learn that someone had invented something to keep fish alive in live wells. This is America, after all, the land of the free and the home of time-sharing condos, where people will do just about anything for a buck. I was starting to get bored

THE BUCK NEVER GOT HERE

with the letter until I read this line, which I promise is an actual quote, "It looks like a miniature scuba system."

Whoa! Miniature scuba systems? I can just imagine watching *Fishing with Bill Dance* on Saturday morning, and after the guest catches a largemouth bass, he turns to Bill and says, "We better get this guy fitted with a vest and air tank right away. As hot as it is, he'll never make it 'till sundown." Yep, when I read that line, I knew, beyond a shadow of a doubt, that I'd get an easy column out of it.

The only problem is that I recently met David Kinser at an outdoor show, and I saw the Oxygen Edge in action. It works, but even more disappointing, it doesn't look like a miniature scuba system.

What it is is a regular oxygen tank with a regulator and hose attached, and on the other end of the hose is what looks like a solid piece of two-inch pipe full of tiny holes, through which the oxygen leaks in tiny bubbles, similar to the Don Ho song. The pipe is dropped into a live well, and the bubbles float to the top, but on the way, they release oxygen into the water. This makes it much easier for the fish to breathe, and they stay alive longer.

To illustrate how a fish feels in a live well without the Oxygen Edge, David put a clothespin on my nose, stuck a straw in my mouth, and told me to breathe through the straw. I only hope you readers appreciate the trouble I go to to keep you on the cutting edge of outdoors technology. I felt like an idiot, and I also had trouble breathing. This proves, of course, that fish in live wells need the Oxygen Edge. David had some fish in an aquarium, and they certainly looked happy.

Which makes me wonder if people who go to oxygen bars, which are very popular in Japan, are as gullible as I thought they were. At an oxygen bar, you pay real, hard-earned money to sit on a stool next to a stranger and breathe oxygen through a hose, which is supposed to make you feel good. I'm sure it makes someone feel good, but it's probably the guy who owns the bar. This sort of thing makes selling a refrigerator to an Eskimo seem downright ethical.

Anyway, if you want live, happy fish, call Oxygenation Systems of Texas. The Oxygen Edge really works, I think, and David is a very nice guy. And if you need some furniture rearranged, call my wife ...

A PLUMB GOOD IDEA

If you, like many Americans, bathe, then you will definitely be interested in this column. You might want to cut it out of the paper and save it, maybe even read it at some point, because it contains an idea I came up with all by myself, by the simple yet effective method of stealing it from someone else. It's a little known fact that most of my original ideas are originally thought up by someone else, which is, I think, probably the best way to have original ideas. It frees your mind up so you can think about other things, like where you left your car keys.

Anyway, this idea contains one of the best ideas I've ever had, so I've been putting off writing about it for a

THE BUCK NEVER GOT HERE

long time, for fear someone will steal it, which is how I got it. But I've decided to give my readers this idea for free, which is exactly what it cost me. Don't thank me; it's my job.

When I take a shower, I always keep a sharp eye out for wild animals. I worry about having a rabid coon or skunk wander into the shower with me and bite me. As hot and dry as it's been this summer, this is a very real possibility.

Perhaps you don't personally have to worry about being attacked by crazed creatures while engaging in acts of personal hygiene. Perhaps the most danger you face when you take a shower is falling and bumping your noggin on the soap dish. Perhaps your shower is located inside your house.

Several years ago, I went on a bowhunt for pigs at John "Mac" McAfee's ranch, which is located somewhere between Fredericksburg and Llano, I think. My friend Royce Laskoskie drove, and I didn't pay a lot of attention to where we went. Anyway, we stayed overnight in the old ranch house on the place, which was equipped with, among other things, an outdoor shower. I availed myself of the shower, and enjoyed it so much I immediately decided I would someday build one at my house.

When I went home and told my wife I wanted to build a shower in our backyard, she responded with her usual positive encouragement. "You're nuts," she said. "Why would you want to build a shower in the backyard when we have a perfectly good one in the bathroom?" I was glad she was so excited about the project, but I put off actually starting on the shower for a while, to make sure her initial enthusiasm didn't wane.

Then, in July of 1995, I came home one day and found my wife washing our boys in the backyard with a hose. Our water comes out of a well, when we're lucky, and is fairly chilly, even during the summer. At first, I thought the boys were wearing blue long handles, but then I noticed that they weren't wearing anything. They didn't look real happy.

Jocelynn (my wife) explained that it was a royal pain to bathe the boys in the bathtub, since it was hot and they made a big mess, not to mention that she had trouble bending over the tub, due to the fact that she was extremely pregnant at the time. I patted her on the shoulder and made sympathy-type noises, and told her she shouldn't be going to all that trouble, and that I was going to do something about it. She immediately brightened up, thinking I meant I would take over the boy-washing duties. Then I hit her with the outdoor shower idea again, extolling its virtues and pointing out that it would be outside, and it would keep her from having to bend over a hot bathtub, and it would have no drain to stop up, etc. It worked, and she gave me the go-ahead.

Building the shower was a little more trouble than I expected, due in large part to the fact that showers contain plumbing. I've figured out the reason the space program is so expensive is because NASA has to hire a bunch of plumbers to build the space shuttles.

THE BUCK NEVER GOT HERE

Plumbing is basically rocket science, on a smaller scale. Plumbers may charge a lot of money, but they're worth every penny. If you don't think so, come take a look at the pipes in, around, under, and over my outdoor shower. But not while I'm using it.

Although we live in the country, my wife insisted the shower have walls, so I built some, but left them open a foot at the bottom, and they're only five feet tall, so I can watch for rabid animals. Jocelynn also insisted on a concrete floor and lights so she can see if there are any snakes around when she goes out there at night. I think that takes a lot of the fun out of it, but we all have to make compromises.

I will admit, however, that the walls have some extra benefits. I've started putting corn out about fifty yards from the shower, and the deer are coming in pretty well, and I'm hoping to set some kind of record by being the first hunter in history to shoot a deer while taking a shower.

As a matter of fact, I've already hunted out of my "wet blind." A few years ago, we had a problem with coons coming in and eating our cat's food, and when my wife noticed one outside one evening, we ran out and ambushed it by hiding in the shower. She held a light while I shot the coon, and then we noticed a small pig close by (he and his family had been rooting up our yard for several weeks) and I shot him too. So the shower does very well as a hunting blind.

I have no doubt this idea will catch on and become very popular. Before long, you'll be seeing pictures in magazines and newspapers of happy, successful hunters posing with their dead deer while wrapped in camouflage towels. I would market the shower/blind myself, but I can't handle the plumbing...

NORTH AMERICA'S GREATEST ATHLETES

ESPN recently decided to compile a list of who they think are the top one hundred North American athletes of the current century (the 1900s). Last week in his newspaper column, Jack Cowan, *San Angelo Standard Times* Editorial Page Editor, gave his own list of who he thinks are the top ten, and why. I was very impressed with Jack's list, although I disagree with everyone on it. As he pointed out in his column, however, everyone thinks their list is right, so it's really a matter of opinion.

I also should mention that I really like Jack Cowan. He's a nice, friendly guy who writes timely, informative articles about current world events and, although he's over forty, still has most of his own hair. So I hate to be too critical, but the fact is his list is, in my opinion, all wrong.

When you get right down to it, though, I'm sure a lot more people would agree with Jack's top ten athletes than mine. He picked people like Muhammad Ali, Michael Jordan, Babe Ruth, Jesse Owens, and Jack Nicklaus. While I will admit all these people were, or are, athletic, I wouldn't put any of them on my top ten list.

The problem, as I see it, is that most people think that games like football, basketball, baseball, hockey,

THE BUCK NEVER GOT HERE

golf, and boxing are sports. They are not. They are children's games. Real sports don't involve balls or short pants. Real sports don't involve referees or timeouts. And you don't see real sports on television much, since real sports aren't practiced in stadiums or arenas.

Now, before I get a lot of angry letters containing beer stains and misspelled words, let me point out that I don't have anything against games like football, basketball, etc. I think they can be very beneficial for kids, and they can help teach values and ethics, as long as they are kept in proper perspective. But games left their proper perspective in North America a long time ago. Professional athletes make so much money they have to stay in shape just to be able to carry their wallets around, and they do it by using their God-given talent to play games. I don't mind them being well paid, but nothing turns my stomach faster than hearing how sad it is that some pro athlete has been injured, can't play anymore, and is now just a normal person like you and me, and must work for a living. Well, so what? Who shouldn't have to work for a living?

The other problem I have with pro athletes is the bad example some of them set for our youth. The night before a recent Super Bowl, an Atlanta Falcon was arrested for trying to solicit sex from an undercover police officer. Michael Irvin was once caught in a motel room with drugs and prostitutes while his family sat at home. The list could go on and on, but the worst part is that, instead of being prosecuted, or at least kicked off the team, these people generally get nothing more

KENDAL HEMPHILL

than a slap on the wrist, which sends a clear message to the young people in America: We don't care how many laws you break, or how immoral you are, as long as you catch enough passes. There are too few Troy Aikmans in pro sports, and too many Michael Irvins.

Cole Younger, who supposedly ran with the Jesse James gang sometimes, came upon a baseball game during the early part of this century and asked what was going on. When told that the game was called baseball, and that it was America's number one sport, he reportedly said, "Shooting is America's number one sport, and always will be." I think he was right, and the statistics still bear this out, so I believe a shooter should be on any top ten list of North American athletes. If the time period in question went back to 1850, I might pick Billy Dixon, for shooting an Indian over 1,500 yards away during the famous fight at Adobe Walls, using a Sharps .50. Or maybe Texas Ranger Captain Jack Hays, for his entire career, but especially his lone stand-off of about a hundred Comanches at Enchanted Rock. Since both of them are disqualified, I would have to pick Marine Gunnery Sergeant Carlos Hathcock, who is still a legend in the armed forces for his exploits as a sniper during the Vietnam War. He spent almost as much time behind enemy lines as the enemy, either alone or with only a spotter, and logged ninety-three confirmed kills, one of them from 2,500 yards. He also won the 1,000-yard National High-Power Rifle Championship at Camp Perry, Ohio, in 1965.

And how about Eddie Rickenbacker, who, as a fighter pilot during World War I, shot down twenty-two German planes, and was the leading American combat pilot of the war. Then in 1942, at age fifty-two, he was forced to ditch his plane in the South Pacific and spent twenty-three days in a raft with six others before being rescued. If that's not athletic, I don't know what is.

My list would also include Alvin York, Roy Benavides, Audie Murphy, John J. Pershing, Lewis Puller, Greg Boyington, and Joe Foss. You'll never hear anything about any of those guys on ESPN. They never hit a home run, or caught a touchdown pass, or made a hole in one. All they did was risk their lives so Babe Ruth, Michael Irvin, and Jack Nicholas could do those things.

And so ESPN could compile a list of the top 100 athletes of the century...

I THINK I COULD BE A WRITER

People often come up to me and say, "You know, I've been thinking about doing some writing. I know lots of stories, and I think I could do a pretty good job of it." They generally say it in the same tone of voice you would use to say, "You know, I think I'll go get a bite to eat," or "You know, I think I'll go change my underwear," as if it were just something you decided to do one day, and you did it.

I always encourage these people. You never know when you might be talking to the next Elmer Kelton. Of course, you also never know when you might be talking to the next Salmon Rushde. I enjoy visiting with these aspiring writers, especially when I talk to one of them after they've tried writing for a while, and they find out it actually involves work.

The guy who wrote *Shoeless Joe,* the book from which the movie *Field of Dreams* was made, was recently in San Angelo for a writers' seminar, and I went to part of it. He said it always irritated him when people who had never done any writing told him they were planning to write a book. He said that at a party a while back, he had been talking to a neurosurgeon, and the doctor said, "I'm going to retire in a couple of years, and I'm planning to write a book."

The guy who wrote *Shoeless Joe* said, "Well, I'm going to retire soon too, and I'm planning to do a little brain surgery."

Since there seem to be so many people out there who are interested in writing, I've decided to offer some guidelines you can go by if you want to give it a shot. I've never had a journalism class in my life, but I've been writing a column of a thousand words or so every week for the past two years with basically nothing to say, so I think I'm qualified here.

You've probably heard a lot of advice, such as: The number one rule about writing is to write about what you know about. This is a lot of sheep drench. If I only wrote about things I know about, I wouldn't have come up with more than three or four columns by now. And those wouldn't have been worth reading.

The truth is most newspaper columnists have to write about all kinds of things, most of which they know nothing about. What they usually do in this situ-

THE BUCK NEVER GOT HERE

ation is find an expert on the subject they're covering and ask him a lot of boring questions. This will work, but I use a slightly different method–I make things up. I think real hard about my topic, and maybe eat a Hershey bar, and then I write whatever pops into my head. This is why I am what is called in the journalism profession a "freelance writer."

Actually, I usually only write about things that have something to do with the outdoors. This is a pretty broad subject, since everything has something to do with the outdoors, including the indoors. All you have to do is compare your subject to what you're really supposed to be writing about.

For instance, if I wanted to write about, say, lawyers, I would relate lawyers in some way to the outdoors. I might start with, "When fishing for really big catfish, it's not too good an idea to use lawyers for bait." Then I might go on and explain why lawyers won't attract catfish, such as the fact that bottom feeders never eat each other.

Another rule you've probably heard is, "Write the way you talk." This is not bad advice, as long as you don't talk like William F. Buckley, Jr. His books read like an encyclopedia, without the excitement.

Another problem with this "rule" is that you may personally be from Alabama. No one can understand Southerners. The good news is that a lot of their accent is lost in print, so reading something they've written is not as bad as listening to them. At least they are more understandable than teenage girls.

Now, before you get all riled up, let me point out that I don't have anything against teenage girls, but I've listened to some of them talk a few times, and it seems that every other word they use is *like*. Also, most of their sentences are questions. This just doesn't look good in print.

A typical teenage girl conversation might go something like this:

First Girl: "Have you, like, seen the new biology teacher? He's, like, soooo cute!"

Second Girl: (Squealing) "Like, I was walking into the gym? With, like, my books? And he, like, came around the corner? And, like, almost ran into me? I was, like, so embarrassed!"

Third Girl: "Like?"

So we can see that, while there are rules you can follow in becoming a writer, most of them are, like, wrong. What you have to do is find your own style, and write the way that's most comfortable for you. And you should bear in mind that in writing, more than any other profession, everybody you meet thinks they can do your job at least as well as you can.

I once saw an NFL wide receiver on a talk show, and he said he'd met a lot of people who thought they could do what he did. After all, all he really had to do was catch a ball. How hard could that be? Anyone could do it.

The pro ball player told the audience, "If you think you could be a wide receiver in the pros, here's what you can do to find out. Invite two of your friends over.

Give one of them a football, and the other a baseball bat. Have the friend with the ball pitch it to you real easy, from about six feet away, but high enough that you have to stretch your arms over your head and stand on your tiptoes to reach it. At the exact moment the ball touches your fingertips, have the other friend hit you in the teeth with the bat as hard as he can. If you can catch the ball nine out of ten times, you can be an NFL wide receiver."

Speaking for myself, I plan to stick to writing. And now, if you'll excuse me, I think I'll go change my underwear...

DOMESTIC TERRORISTS

For years we've been amused by the ridiculous complaints and accusations of animal rights groups such as people for the ethical treatment of animals (peta), Friends of Animals, the Humane Society, and others. They've tried to encourage our young people to drink beer instead of milk, cried foul about casino patrons playing tick-tack-toe against chickens, vilified Burger King because their veggie burgers are cooked on the same grill with meat patties, and filed lawsuits against McDonald's for labeling French fries and hash browns as vegetarian items, because they're fried in vegetable oil that contains traces of beef essence.

Hardly a week goes by that people with common sense don't get a chuckle from the antics of these supposedly well-meaning imbeciles. We ignore their inane babblings and smile at their suggestions concerning relocation of prairie dogs. We shake our heads at their attempts to control deer population through contraception, and we just about busted a gut when a couple of them sued the state of New Jersey because they hit a deer with their car.

The problem is they're not funny anymore. They're dangerous.

The basic premise of animal rights groups is that animals are just as important as people, if not more so. Alex Pacheco, former director of peta, said, "We feel that animals have the same rights as retarded children." peta's president, Ingrid Newkirk, said, "Six million Jews died in concentration camps, but 6 billion broiler chickens will die this year in slaughterhouses."

Chris De Rose, director of Last Chance for Animals, said, "If the death of one rat cured all diseases, it wouldn't make any difference to me." A rat's life, in other words, is as important as the lives of countless people.

Many people think of the Humane Society as a group interested only in helping animals that have been abandoned or abused, certainly not a radical organization. But its vice president, Michael W. Fox, said, "The life of an ant and that of my child should be granted equal consideration." Not much doubt where Fox stands.

These attitudes are disturbing, but most of us have not associated animal rights activists with actual violence in the past. All that has changed. Pacheco, who is now head of an animal rights fund-raising company,

THE BUCK NEVER GOT HERE

recently said, "Arson, property destruction, burglary, and theft are 'acceptable crimes' when used for the animal cause." These people have no regard for the property or safety of other humans.

One of the main problems in combating these space cadets is that they're seen as people who are sincerely trying to do the Right Thing. They are not. Their efforts are aimed, not at obtaining rights for animals, but at controlling the lives of the rest of us. We need to wake up and smell the litter box. They want to take away our freedom, and maybe our lives.

On September 11, 2001, the day of the terrorist attacks in New York and Washington D.C., the Earth Liberation Front and its sister group, the Animal Liberation Front, took "credit" for burning a McDonald's in Tucson. Nine days later, the ALF set fire to the Coulston Foundation primate-research facility, and claims to have been the group that set fire to two meat trucks in New York in March, 2001, and placed other incendiary devices beneath trucks in Canada in 2000.

FBI special agent David Szady said, "Make no mistake about it; by any sense or any definition, (ELF) is a domestic-terrorism group." ALF uses the same tactics, as do many other groups.

The problem has reached the point where even our federal government recognizes the threat. On February 12, 2002, U.S. Congress held a hearing on eco-terrorism, at which Craig Rosebraugh, former spokesman for ELF, was called to testify. When asked about the 137 attacks the ELF took credit for during 2001, including the firebombing of a Vail ski resort, which resulted in $12 million in damages, Rosebraugh pled the Fifth Amendment more than fifty times.

ELF's website opens with a picture of a burning building—the direct work of its members. The first page contains an article entitled "Setting Fires with Electrical Timers–an Earth Liberation Front Guide." There is no question that David Szady is correct.

David Barbarash of the ALF sells books online that contain instructions for criminal activity. The ELF and ALF brag that they have caused $45 million in damages since 1997.

The 2002 national animal rights conference was held in Washington, D.C., June 28–July 3. One of the highlights was a speech by Captain Paul Watson, founder and president of the Sea Shepherd Conservation Society. Watson quoted Timothy McVeigh, who said he considered dead women and children to be collateral damage, a by-product of war.

Watson was also quoted as saying, "There are 30 million plus species on this planet. They're all earthlings. They're all equal. And some are more equal than others, I admit. Earthworms are far more valuable than people." He also said, "There's nothing wrong with being a terrorist, as long as you win."

Last June, peta hired Gary Yourofsky as its National Lecturer, planning to have him tour the nation and speak to educators and students. Yourofsky founded Animals Deserve Adequate Protection Today and Tomorrow, and is a strong advocate of terrorism. He

THE BUCK NEVER GOT HERE

has a tattoo displaying the symbols of the ELF, and once said that if an animal abuser were killed in the process of burning down a research lab, "I would unequivocally support that."

We are involved in a war against eco-terrorists, and one of the main problems we face is the difficulty in recognizing the enemy. Some of these groups, such as the Humane Society of the United States, are viewed as benign animal lovers. Many of them adopt names that conjure images of cuddly kittens and playful puppies in order to lure honest people into opening up their wallets. When all else fails, they lie. peta, for instance, claims to eschew violence, yet the organization makes large donations to ALF.

This is a war we will not win unless, and until, we acknowledge the fact that animal rights activists are people-hating criminals, no less a threat to the American way of life than Al Qaeda. Even those groups that don't actually condone violence are guilty, since they encourage citizens to become involved in the overall cause. There is no middle ground left.

No sensible, intelligent person abuses animals, or tolerates those who do. But animal abuse is not the issue here. The issue is people abuse, and the problem has become epidemic in America. Unless we stand up against it, we deserve to lose.

We've laughed at the animal rights wackos long enough. It's time to start taking them seriously...

A CONVENIENT LIE

Al Gore may not be the sharpest croquet ball in the set, but he's at least smart enough to know that if you want to get people to give you their money, you have to offer them a solution to a problem. It really doesn't matter whether the problem is real or imagined, as long as the dollars they give you are the real kind. If you tell them there is no problem, then there is no money.

Yes, we've talked about global warming before, but it's kind of like one of those kids' punching bags with the picture of a clown on the front. You knock it down and it just pops right back up, asking for another swat. And it never quits smiling. It enjoys getting smacked.

But just to set the record straight, I want to point out that in my last column about this subject, I admitted that I really do believe global warming exists, and that it's happening right now, almost everywhere. I even tried to worry about it some, but I got distracted over Easter weekend, when the snow was piling up in central Texas so deep kids were building snowmen and making snow ice cream. It's hard to ponder the demise of earth due to excessive heat while you're getting hit with snowballs in April.

Of course, the fact that it snowed in central Texas at Easter is not proof that global warming isn't happening, any more than a heat wave in December is proof that it is. That's just one of those strange things that happens in Texas sometimes, like Ann Richards being elected governor, or your sink drain stopping up. It's unpleasant, but you have to deal with it and go on.

THE BUCK NEVER GOT HERE

What I don't believe is that humans are causing global warming through blatant use of aerosol deodorant, gasoline exhaust, excessive belching, or anything else. I think the cycle of gradual warming and cooling of the planet is caused by natural changes in ocean currents, which are affected by lots of factors, including fluctuation of salinity in the water. And I'm not the only one who thinks this way.

William Gray, an emeritus professor at Colorado State University, agrees with me. Well, OK, to be totally honest, the ocean current salinity thing was his idea to begin with, but I don't see any need to split hairs here. The main thing is to stay focused on the problem and what needs to be done about it. Which is, ah, nothing.

Gray is the absolute top dog, head cheese, big enchilada in the entire u.s. of a. when it comes to predicting hurricanes and other major weather events. His annual hurricane forecasts are awaited with bated breath, crossed legs, and tapping feet by the horn-rimmed glasses and pocket protector crowd. There isn't anyone who knows more about big storms than this guy. So I'm forced to bow to his expertise.

At the recent National Hurricane Conference in New Orleans, Gray addressed the nation's top meteorologists and emergency management specialists. He told them, basically, that Al Gore was full of guacamole. He called Al a "gross alarmist" and said Al's claim that storms have gotten worse since the 1970s isn't true. So I guess he called Al a liar too, although calling a politician a prevaricator is like saying the Mississippi River is damp. Not exactly a shocker.

Al's documentary, *An Inconvenient Truth,* claims earth is headed south on a greased pole. The idea is that humans are ruining the planet with greenhouse gasses like carbon dioxide, and unless we do something about it, we're in deep trouble. But Gray, who evidently doesn't hold a candle to Al in the fundraising department, says that's a bunch of hooey. When asked about Al's predictions of horrendous flooding and other disastrous weather events, Gray said, "He's one of these guys that preaches the end of the world type of things. I think he's doing a great disservice and he doesn't know what he's talking about."

So Gray is pretty critical of Al, but I don't think he's adequately considered the situation. Al is trying to win the democratic nomination for the presidential race, and that takes money. And if you come out and tell folks everything is fine, they will inconsiderately fail to donate huge wads of legal tender to your campaign fund. And that doesn't help anyone. Except maybe the citizens of the country, and who cares about them?

Gray says the current cycle of warming oceans, which is causing recent hurricane activity, is going to start going the other way in five to ten years. But then, by that time, we'll all be on mopeds and bicycles, and smelling each other's BO, and Al will claim his movie caused the reduction of poisonous fumes, which in turn saved the planet.

But, hey, Al's a politician. Saving the planet is his job. Well, that and playing croquet…

AUTHOR'S FAVORITES

UNCLE RAY WOULDN'T HAVE WANTED A SAD TRIBUTE

It's never pleasant to lose someone you love. The funeral of a family member, while a necessary farewell and show of respect, is always a sad event. I have often thought it shouldn't be that way, that we should be able to celebrate someone's life without feeling sorry for ourselves for having lost them, especially when they've lived a long, full, happy life. My great uncle, Ray Engdahl, lived that kind of life.

Uncle Ray was my grandfather's baby brother, born in July, 1914. A life of hard work had already worn him down quite a bit by the time I came along, and he was never in what I would call really good health. He started using a cane when I was a kid. But, as far back as I can remember, I don't think I ever saw him unhappy. I can still see him sitting in a chair on his porch, both hands on the top of his cane, looking over his glasses at me and grinning. Matter of fact, I can't remember seeing him one time in my life that he wasn't grinning.

Of course, he laughed a lot too, but his grin was special. Everyone who ever knew him knew that grin. He enjoyed a good joke, or a good hunting or fishing story, and it seemed like he wore that grin so he'd be ready to laugh when the occasion arose, and it arose pretty often around Uncle Ray. You probably couldn't find anyone who enjoyed life more than he did.

Maybe that's why it seemed so strange to me, last week at his funeral, to be so sad. Sure, I'm going to miss him. I'm going to miss his stories. I'm going to miss his ribbing. I'm going to miss his laugh. I'm especially going to miss his grin. But his funeral was the first time in my life that I was in Uncle Ray's presence that I wasn't happy about it. It just wasn't right.

All his life, Uncle Ray was an outdoors kind of guy. He was born and lived his whole life in the house his father built near Rochelle, Texas. As a farmer, he spent most of his time out from under a roof. He hunted and fished as often as he could, and he never lost his sense of humor, not even at the end. When his preacher, Kenneth Barr, went to visit him in the hospital just before he died, Uncle Ray couldn't talk, but he gave Ken that grin and pretended to cast and reel a fishing rod.

THE BUCK NEVER GOT HERE

Most of my memories of Uncle Ray involve dove hunting on the home place at Rochelle. Once, about 1988, we were hunting near a set of cattle pens on the place with several other guys, and Uncle Ray shot a dove that fell inside one of the pens. He told me to go get it for him, and when I climbed over the fence, I found that a rat snake had the dove's head in his mouth and was crawling off with it. Uncle Ray told me to shoot the snake and bring the dove back. Its head was all wet, but when I pitched it down in front of him, it got up and flew off again. Several shots were fired at it as it flew away, but it just kept going. Uncle Ray looked at me with that grin and said, "You'd just as well not tell anybody about that. They won't believe it anyway." He was right, nobody has ever believed it, but it happened just the same.

My three boys rode with my parents from the funeral home to the Rochelle cemetery to bury Uncle Ray, and as they drove through Rochelle, my mother pointed to the Rochelle school and told the boys, "Look, there's the building where I went to school."

Courtland, the seven-year-old, said, "Wow! And it's still standing?"

A minute later my dad said, "Look, boys, there's the cemetery."

Leret, who is three, asked, "What's a cemetery?"

Dad said, "That's where people are buried."

Paden, five, asked, "Is it full?" I have no idea why that occurred to him.

Dad tried to explain cemeteries to the boys. He said, "If more room is needed, the cemetery can be expanded, but usually, after a while, the younger folks move away, and decide they want to be buried somewhere else. So there's not much danger of running out of room."

Paden asked, "How do the dead people tell you they want to be buried somewhere else?"

A very good question, I thought. I told my wife recently that when I die I want to be buried in one of those huge Igloo ice chests, the kind that have the split lids, so you can open half of it at a time. I'll bet an Igloo would do better in a blowing-out-of-the-back-of-the-pickup test than one of those high-dollar caskets.

Or I could go with Canuck's Sportsman's Memorials, Inc., a Des Moines, Iowa, business that specializes in some diverse funerary options. Owner Jay W. "Canuck" Knudsen, Sr., does lots of interesting things with cremated remains, like sealing them inside fishing bobbers and hand-carved duck decoys. If you'd like to go out with a bang, Knudsen will load your ashes into shotgun shells and fire them at the game animal of your choice. He recently did that with the remains of one of his clients, shooting 12-gauge shotgun shells containing the deceased's ashes at a 400-pound black bear in Saskatchewan.

To me, that sounds like about as good a way to go as any, although I think I'd rather have my ashes shot at doves flying over the old cattle pens at Rochelle. I kind of wish I'd suggested that to Uncle Ray, but if I had, he'd have probably given me that famous grin and said,

"Naw, you'd just miss all the birds, and if you managed to knock one down, some old rat snake would probably get off with it."

CHARLY MCTEE—THE VOICE OF FRIENDSHIP

Someone once said, "One doesn't make friends; one recognizes them." I never really understood that statement until I met Charly McTee. I had always believed a real friendship needed time to develop, but then, I'd never met anyone like Charly.

It seems like I've known Charly ever since I can remember, but I haven't. I met him in January, 1996, at the Texas Outdoor Writers Association annual meeting. I wasn't a member at that time, but I wanted to meet some of the folks who were, specifically Charly, so I drove over a hundred miles on icy roads to San Angelo and hung around the hotel feeling like a fish in a feedlot. Until Charly walked up and stuck out his hand.

You couldn't visit with Charly and feel like you belonged anywhere else. He was comfortable, like the easy chair in your living room, the one you sit in every day and don't offer to guests because it's yours. That chair gives you a sense of place, of contentment, and Charly did that for me. He made me feel as though I were worth listening to. In just a few minutes, he put me at ease and made me a part of the group. A group I really wasn't a part of.

I guess the most important thing about Charly, to me at least, was that he was Charly. Not Mister McTee. Nobody called him Mr. McTee. It didn't fit.

KENDAL HEMPHILL

Not because it was too big or too small, it was just...
the wrong color maybe. Charly was a lot of things, but
he wasn't uppity. He was about as down to earth and
easy-going as anybody I've ever known.

Probably the reason Charly's friendliness was so
impressive to me was because I'd been listening to him
all my life on the radio. He was the voice of the outdoors, and millions of people, over the years, listened
to his outdoor radio show. When you were turning
the dial, trying to find a station, and you came across
Charly's voice, you stopped. Like Mel Gibson in *Lethal
Weapon*, when he was channel surfing for a TV station and came across the Three Stooges, and threw the
remote control over his shoulder. Charly's voice was
like a magnet—once I heard it, I couldn't stop listening. I can't remember any of the advice or information I
ever heard from him, but I can still hear his voice in my
head. I'll be hearing it for the rest of my life. I couldn't
forget it even if I wanted to, and I don't want to.

That voice. It was a voice that instilled in its lis-
teners the sense of down-homeyness, of we're-all-in-
this-togetherness that Roosevelt's "Fireside Chats"
were supposed to do. It was a voice that came through
the radio and sat down beside you and put its arm
around you, and made you forget your troubles for a
while. It was a voice that took you with it to fish a
lake you'd never seen, or float a river you'd never heard
of. It was a voice that let you smell the coffee mixed
with woodsmoke, and hold out your icy fingers to the
campfire and feel the tingle as they thawed. It was a

THE BUCK NEVER GOT HERE

voice that made you feel as though it were talking only to you, and no one else was listening. It wasn't just a voice... it was a friend.

It was that voice, I think, that captivated my boys the last time I saw Charly. They'd only met him once, several months before, and then only briefly, so my wife and I snuck them up to his room in the hospital in San Antonio, where he was undergoing cancer treatments. Three- and five-year-olds were not allowed in there, but they'd picked out a coloring book and some crayons for him, and we wanted them to be able to give them to him themselves.

Apprehensive about their surroundings, the boys were a little shy at first, but in a few minutes, they were crawling up on Charly's bed, laughing, and making themselves at home. Every night from then on, when they said their prayers, the boys prayed for Charly to get better. Every night.

When my wife and I arrived in Corpus Christi for the 1997 TOWA conference, I still entertained a faint hope that Charly had maybe gotten better, and that I might see him there. When we learned he had passed on a few days before, I felt like turning around and going home. I'm glad we didn't. I met several people over the weekend who had been Charly's friends for many years, and I learned a great deal more about this man with the golden voice.

As I listened to all the "Charly stories," I came to realize what a special guy he was, and how lucky I had been to have known him at all. I also became envious of those around me. They talked of memories I'll never have, and the more I listened, the harder it was for me to believe that, although I talked with Charly on the phone several times and exchanged letters with him, I only actually saw him twice. But Charly was a giver, and he gave me more in those two meetings than many people I've known all my life. I only wish I'd had a chance to give some back.

No, there'll never be another Charly, but as much as he accomplished in his life, and as much as he did for those around him, maybe one Charly was enough.

When we got home, I sat the boys down and told them about Charly. When they said their prayers that night, they prayed for Charly's family. I wonder if they'll ever know how many people they were praying for…

A TALE OF TWO FLAGS

When you see the black-and-white picture of the six Marines raising the American flag on a barren, windswept hilltop, you don't have to ask where it was taken. You know the scene occurred on the tiny South Pacific island of Iwo Jima on February 23, 1945. That snapshot, taken by Associated Press photographer Joe Rosenthal, is the most reproduced photograph in history.

More u.s. Marines earned the Medal of Honor during the battle for Iwo Jima than in any other u.s. battle. The thirty-six days of fighting saw the loss of over 6,800 American fighting men. Almost all of the 22,000 Japanese soldiers on the island were killed.

THE BUCK NEVER GOT HERE

When those six Marines (Ira Hayes, Franklin Sousley, John Bradley, Harlon Block, Michael Strank, and Rene Gagnon) hoisted Old Glory on Mount Suribachi that gray morning, they raised up the hopes of an entire nation with it. They showed the world that America would not be defeated, that freedom was worth our blood, our tears, the very lives of the best of us.

That picture fills half the background on the computer screen I'm writing this column on. The other half is filled with a picture of another flag-raising, one that occurred September 11, 2001, atop the remains of the World Trade Center towers. Fifty-six years and nine thousand miles apart, the two events are alike in many ways.

Raised by firefighters instead of Marines, the flag that went up September 11 stood for the same hopes and values as did the one on Mount Suribachi. More importantly, it accomplished the same purpose. It told our enemies, those who would destroy what that ensign represents, that America is more than a collection of buildings and people, more than a democratic society of free citizens, more than the ink on a pile of yellowed documents lying in our National Archives Building. America is us. And we're still here.

Dan McWilliams and his fellow firefighters of Brooklyn's Ladder 157 had been digging for survivors in the wreckage of the WTC towers for several hours when they were ordered to evacuate the area. WTC building seven was about to come down. Dan was on his way out when he noticed a yacht docked in back of the World Financial Center. There was an American flag flying from it.

223

After commandeering the flag, Dan was on his way back to the evacuation area when he met George Johnson, also of Ladder 157, and said, "Gimme a hand, will ya, George?" Billy Eisengrein, of Brooklyn's Rescue 2, fell in to help.

They found a pole sticking out of the rubble on West Street, about twenty feet off the ground, and went to work to hoist the national colors. About that time, Tom Franklin, a staff photographer for Hackensack, New Jersey's *The Record* newspaper, saw what was going on. He captured the moment on film, and did for three of New York's Bravest what Joe Rosenthal had done for six U.S. Marines fifty-six years before.

Like the flag on Iwo Jima, the one raised at the WTC was erected on ground bought with the blood of the comrades-in-arms of those who put it up. They weren't soldiers or Marines, but they were in just as much of a war as Strank's men, albeit a different kind of war. Thousands of Americans lost their lives on September 11, just as thousands died on Iwo Jima in February and March of 1945. Most of them were civilians, true, and many came from foreign countries, but Strank himself was born in Czechoslovakia.

Sadly, three of Mount Suribachi's flag raisers, Harlon Block, Franklin Sousley, and Michael Strank, all died in later battles on Iwo Jima. Hayes, Bradley, and Gagnon came home to a hero's welcome and were honored all over the country.

Which brings us to what is probably the most glaring similarity between the events of February 23, 1945

THE BUCK NEVER GOT HERE

and September 11, 2001. Bradley, Hayes, and Gagnon didn't want to be called heroes. Neither do McWilliams, Johnson, and Eisengrein.

President Truman told Ira Hayes, when he visited the White House, "You are an American hero." He never felt like one.

Hayes later asked, "How could I feel like a hero when only five men in my platoon of forty-five survived, when only twenty-seven men in my company of 250 managed to escape death or injury?" The three firefighters could make a similar query.

Rene Gagnon, the man who carried the flag up Mount Suribachi, was modest about his accomplishments throughout his life. John Bradley maintained he wasn't a hero, and he wouldn't talk about his achievements. His own children didn't even know he had helped raise the flag until after his death in 1994. Bradley said the real heroes were the men who gave their lives for their country.

McWilliams, Johnson, and Eisengrein would tell you the heroes of September 11 are those who gave their lives to try to save others. They won't accept phone calls from the media, and their fellow firefighters are being very careful to keep them from being pestered.

I finally got hold of Dan McWilliams in late September 2001, and spoke to him as one firefighter to another. I told him I just wanted to say thanks for raising the flag. He said it was no big deal, but that all the guys up there just needed a shot in the arm. I asked him if there was anything we could do for them, and he said, "Just keep praying."

The third verse of "America the Beautiful" says, "Oh beautiful for heroes proved in liberating strife, who more than self their country loved, and mercy more than life."

Our country continues the fight against terrorism, and there are likely to be more heroes. Some we will hear about, some we will not. But wherever our troops go in the world, when they raise our flag, it will be the same star spangled banner, and it will stand for the same things.

America will remain the land of the free because it is the home of the brave ...

DAD

The cold winter sky seemed to press down on us, threatening snow, stiffening our fingers, and invading our lungs with every breath. We had been walking for a couple of hours, and night was not far off. We were headed back toward the pickup, with little chance of making it before we ran out of daylight. Even so, every time I whispered and pointed to a log, Dad stopped, and we sat and rested for a few minutes.

I was probably seven or eight, excited to be on my first real hunt with my father, instead of just riding around in the pickup with the heater running, looking for deer out the window.

I remember thinking how neat it was to be able to get Dad to stop whenever I wanted him to. We'd

THE BUCK NEVER GOT HERE

whisper for a while, Dad still hoping for a shot, and then he'd ask if I was ready, and we'd get up and walk some more.

Like most Texas kids, I learned about hunting and fishing from my father, begging to go every time he left the house. Having a brother almost four years older, who got to go a lot sooner than I did, made things seem terribly unfair. Still, Dad took me whenever he could, and I can't remember a time when he went hunting or fishing without one or both of us tagging along.

The three of us went on our first river camping trip when I was about six. We loaded up and went fishing in the Llano River and slept in the back of the pickup. We didn't catch much, but Dad had brought hamburgers, which he flavored with river onions and cooked over an open fire.

I can remember worrying how he knew it was OK to eat those things he pulled out of the ground, but I can also remember how good those hamburgers tasted. I decided Dad knew what he was doing.

I remember listening to my dad and brother talking while lying in the back of the pickup, looking up at the stars. Dad pointed out the Dippers and the North Star, which was about the extent of his astronomical expertise.

That was plenty for me. Being able to identify the moon is good enough for a six-year-old, and I was happy just to be included on an adventure with the big boys. Life doesn't get any better.

The first time I got to go hunting alone I was ten, and Dad gave me some loaded-down shells he'd found for his

.243. He showed me where to sit the day before the season opened, and pointed out where I would see a deer.

I huddled under my bush the next morning, shivering with cold, barely able to stay awake after having been too excited to sleep the night before. When I could finally see, I looked where Dad had pointed and, sure enough, in a few minutes, a doe stepped out and gave me an easy, broadside shot.

If my dad had told me the sun was going to come up in the west, I would have bet the farm on it.

He met me halfway to the house, almost as excited as I was, and helped me field dress my deer and take it to the barn. When I asked him why he wasn't hunting, he pointed to the rifle I was holding and said, "That's the only gun I've got." I felt a good three inches high.

I couldn't believe Dad had passed up hunting on the first day of the season just so I could go alone.

But then, Dad sacrificed for his family all his life. Teachers don't make a lot of money now, but in the 60s and 70s, the pay scale was even worse. We never had a lot, but if someone did without, it was usually Dad. I can remember dove hunts when he spotted for us empty-handed because there weren't enough shotguns to go around.

Dad grew up fast, having lost his older brother at age twelve, and his father five years later. He attended Abilene Christian College, at the same time trying to help his mother and two little sisters on the family farm at Lohn, Texas. I guess he got used to doing without, having known no other way.

THE BUCK NEVER GOT HERE

Now that Dad's gone, I find myself wondering who's going to pick me up when I stumble, dust off the seat of my pants, and get me going again. I realize how much I depended on him, and how much I took him for granted.

This Christmas, and from now on, give your children something money can't buy: your time. A father's most important job is being a dad to his kids. Anyone can be a father, but it takes a special guy to be a dad.

Outdoorsmen and women participate in numerous programs that benefit their states and the communities they live in. Hunters for the Hungry distributes donated meat to needy citizens. The Hunt of a Lifetime foundation enables terminally ill children to experience the outdoors in ways that otherwise would not be possible. Other sportsmen's groups donate time and money to various humanitarian efforts, and without the revenue created by the sale of hunting and fishing licenses, there would be no such thing as wildlife conservation.

Still, there is no substitute for a father who teaches the traditions, values, and ethics of sportsmanship to his children. We owe it to the next generation to pass on our hunting and fishing heritage, so the outdoors will still be there for others to enjoy. The best way to do that is father to son or daughter.

That first hunt with Dad? The sky was dark long before we got out of the woods that day, and snowflakes were falling by the time we got back to the pickup. I wasn't worried. I knew we'd get back OK, and I was snug and warm anyway. Dad had taken off his coat and put me on his back, and then put his coat back on over me.

He couldn't button it in front, but at least one of us was warm and dry. Seems like that kind of thing happened a lot, over the years.

That's what dads do ...

JUST THE OTHER DAY

He was born just the other day, during a war that was taking place halfway around the world. Proof, maybe, that life would still go on, that good things happen in a world where so much bad occurs. The beginning of something impossible to understand or describe, something that has to be experienced, lived.

> "A boy is a piece of existence quite separate from all things else and deserves a separate chapter in the natural history of man."
>
> —Henry Ward Beecher

After a while, I realized he was a person. Maybe I had viewed a child as a sort of pet, at least until it was old enough to talk and go around without diapers. But this one, being present all the time, showed me he was much more than a dog or cat.

> "Two small arms to hold you tight, two small feet to run, two small eyes full of love for you, one small son."
>
> —Author unknown

THE BUCK NEVER GOT HERE

Just the other day, as I was leaving to go somewhere, he held out his arms for a hug. For the first time I realized I was important to him. He wanted to be with me, to do things with me; he wanted us to spend time together. I'd had no idea.

He squeezed me around the neck, and things changed. Life changed. Like it or not, this small person and I were inextricably entwined. Like marshmallows in hot chocolate, impossible to ever completely separate.

Of course, he had known that all along. I had just learned it.

> "Boys are found everywhere—on top of, underneath, inside of, climbing on, swinging from, running around or jumping to ... A boy is Truth with dirt on its face, Beauty with a cut on its finger, Wisdom with bubble gum in its hair, and the Hope of the future with a frog in its pocket."
>
> —Alan Marshall Beck

Suddenly, because of this little boy, I saw things unnoticed for decades. Bugs became valuable entomological specimens to be gathered and studied. Snakes and spiders were no longer unpleasant pests to be immediately disposed of. Cows, sheep, horses, dogs— all had to be watched, smelled, touched, tasted. All had to be experienced.

KENDAL HEMPHILL

> "Boy defined: Nature's answer to that false belief
> that there is no such thing as perpetual motion."
>
> —Arthur unknown

And frogs. Well, catching a frog was the equivalent of finding the pot of gold at the end of the rainbow. Nothing is as valuable to a boy as a frog, to be held, pocketed, petted, and made to hop. Lizards, though also wonderful, are difficult to obtain and more difficult to keep captive. And frogs have such a friendly, personable appearance. To a boy.

> "God made a world out of His dreams, of magic mountains, oceans and streams, prairies and plains, and wooded land. Then paused and thought, 'I need someone to stand on top of the mountains, to conquer the seas, explore the plains, and climb the trees. Someone to start out small and grow sturdy and strong like a tree.' And so He created boys, full of spirit and fun to explore and conquer, to romp and run with dirty faces and banged-up chins, with courageous hearts and boyish grins. And when He had completed the task He'd begun, He surely said, 'That's a job well done.'"
>
> —Author unknown

Just the other day, the boy turned five years old. I gave him his first knife, a little Swiss Army model, to be wielded only under close parental supervision. His face showed this was quite a satisfactory development, as he

THE BUCK NEVER GOT HERE

pulled out the various instruments and tried each one. Every boy needs a Swiss Army knife.

> "And he grew and grew strong as a boy must grow who does not know that he is learning any lessons, and who has nothing in the world to think of except things to eat."
>
> —Rudyard Kipling

His eighth birthday was just the other day, when he got a Red Ryder BB gun. Armed now with the tools necessary to become a great Nimrod, he set forth on Backyard Safaris after Dangerous Game. At night, our home now enjoyed much better protection.

Just the other day, he shot his first deer, no doubt the most bittersweet experience in a young boy's life. Respect for the animal tempers the joy of accomplishment, and lets the boy know this is not an act lightly undertaken, nor cavalierly dismissed. Along with the power to provide for a family comes the responsibility to be a good steward of God's creatures.

> "There comes a time in every rightly constructed boy's life when he has a raging desire to go somewhere and dig for hidden treasure."
>
> —Mark Twain

Just the other day, we went on our first overnight father/son float trip down the river. Time is suspended on the river, the world quietly waits elsewhere, and adventure is always just around the next bend. We turned over in the rapids, camped on a sandbar, cooked chili over a driftwood fire, and slept under the stars. He paddled his boat all the way, insisting he wasn't tired.

At the take-out, I asked him why he was bringing the small, smooth river rock with us. It was just a stone, no different from the thousands of others within sight. He said he would take it home and put it on his dresser and keep it, and it would remind him of the best time he'd ever had. I turned away to tie the boats down.

That was just the other day; now he teeters on the brink of manhood. Today he is in between, with feet too big and pants too short. He becomes more brilliant by the hour, while I lapse rapidly into senility.

Tomorrow, he will be gone. He will leave home, get an education, marry, and start a family. And when he has a child of his own, I will hold the baby, and my son will look at me strangely when I say, "It was just the other day, you know, that I held you like this…"

CPSIA information can be obtained
at www.ICGtesting.com
Printed in the USA
FFOW05n1657210816